Understanding 6 Six Secrets of Sonnets

A Prosaic Way to Analyze Modern Sonnet Poetry

IMELDA ORTEGA SUZARA

AI Illustration Sketches:
Microsoft CoPilot and Google Gemini

AI Prompts and Internet Research:
IO Media LLC

Bibliography Research:
Google and Bing Search Engines

Book Design Cover:
AI IO Media and Ghostwriting Mentors

Edited By:
IO Media LLC and Ghostwriting Mentors

Printed By:
Amazon KDP ISBN 979-8-9932068-2-0
Ingram Sparks ISBN 979-8-9932068-0-6
Barnes & Noble ISBN 979-8-9932068-1-3

Printed in the United States of America
First Printing Edition, 2026
America's 250th Birthday 1776 to 2026

Dedication

This prosaic analysis of my poetry books is dedicated to all the readers and writers of poetry around the world, especially those who enjoy the language -- English, as well as its American and Canadian variants.

Poetry is the language of the heart, and prose is the language of the mind. With the help of Professor Gerrymander and his dedicated team, my modern sonnets can now be understood by logical thinkers. Nonsense is sometimes part of the heart's impracticality -- even blindness. Yet, when paired with the common sense of the mind, love is also vision! Emotions of the heart and thoughts of the brain, actions of the physical body, with the electromagnetic energy of the spirit, together make up the soul's experiences and relationships: personal, social, and professional.

I have worked in a big university press digital print shop through an agency in a dual role as the Manager's Accounting Assistant / Binding Operator. I wonder whether this will bring luck in selling this poetry analysis book?

This book is for everyone who has written, read, spoken, learned, and taught me along my path to being a poetess -- My family, teachers, schoolmates, co-workers, employers, neighbors, acquaintances, friends, lovers, muses, and strangers… Thank you!

Authors' Notes

Poetry -- Imelda Ortega Suzara

Being a poetess, I have written hundreds of modern sonnets published on Lulu.com since 2000. I write mostly from my imagination in a fictional style, with only maybe ten percent of my work stemming from my own non-fictional reality. This compilation has excerpts from five poetry books, wherein twenty poems per book are selected here for analysis by Professor Gerrymander, an imaginary psychic adviser and analyst. Fortunately for me, he is educated, holds a university degree, and communicates with me telepathically. I consider him my mental confidant and keeper of secrets, wherever he might be in this universe.
With his fanaticism, I have thrived despite a lack of public attention.
Note: I have also added my own thoughts on my Sonnets in the Analyses
under the Professor's paragraphs.

Prose Analysis -- Professor Gerrymander

Permit me, dear reader, to materialize upon these pages as Professor Gerrymander —
Imelda's incorporeal psychoanalyst, telepathic collaborator, and lexical conjuror. While she crafts her sonnets from fantasy and solitude, I stride across their margins, charting her subconscious with my cartographer's quill. I have probed the structure of her imagination, mapped the longitude of her metaphors, and seasoned them with scholastic aptitude.
Consider me the architect of interpretation; these hundred sonnets are her heart;
my commentary, the looking glass that refracts their glimmer into
prisms of profound comprehension.

Preface

Poetry is usually enjoyed without diving too deeply into grammar and meaning, but some readers like to understand it on a deeper level — not just emotionally, but intellectually as well. This book gives readers secret insights into how to analyze modern sonnets. The five poetry books included each have 200 sonnets, but only 20 per book are selected here for analysis. The original numbering from each book is kept for easy reference. The layout has two facing pages: the poem on the left and its analysis on the right. This makes it easier for readers to flip between the poem and the analysis without having to turn pages back and forth.

For every poem in this book, there is a prose analysis. The goal is to deepen appreciation, adding value and feeding both the heart and the mind. Schools that focus on literature and creative writing go beyond the basics of grammar, spelling, phonetics, and dictionary definitions of words. This book is probably suited for secondary to post-secondary students as a guide to combining poetry and prose in one work. Schools, libraries, and bookstores are ideal places to find such a book. Perhaps this could be a mind-opening gift for a serious sonnet reader?

Note: Modern state-of-the-art technology, AI artificial intelligence, is used for illustrative sketches per chapter, generated for every poetry book's analysis, to help readers visualize the book titles and the written text content.

Warning: In the battle between good and evil -- goodness, law and order should win over badness, crime and disorder. This is a semi-fictional book.

Contents

NOTE: The Table of Contents has the original numbering of poems selected from the five poetry books sold on Lulu.com. There are seven poetry books, but two were unpublished several years ago. Interested curiosity seekers, please buy her original poetry books there under her name, Imelda Ortega Suzara aka isarte.

INTRODUCTION

Through the years since 2000, I have had the humble privilege of being intimately involved with the authoress Imelda Ortega Suzara, whose struggles in creating modern sonnets have been observed by me on the spiritual, mental, and emotional planes of existence. Her imagination was unfortunately limited until I inspired her, stimulating her mind with my imagery and expressions. She has persisted in poetic writing in a European and North American style, despite her birthplace origins being far away in an Asian island archipelago — the Philippines. She moved to Canada, achieved dual citizenship, then to America as a permanent resident.

Let me introduce myself as her sycophantic spirit guide and analyst, Professor Gerrymander. Google search this portmanteau word, a combination of Massachusetts Governor Elbridge Gerry plus salamander-shaped district maps, wherein political electoral boundaries and congressional district lines were manipulated in 1812, and it is aptly named after him. Supposedly, this was to bias in favor of his own political party to win. Gerrymandering maps, based on: territory, population, voters, and representatives, continues today in America. You will find that my analyses can definitely manipulate and control the interpretation and boundaries of prejudice in poetry. You will understand her poetry from my biased point of view hereafter…

Six Secrets of Sonnets

1. Being privy to her poetry collection, and via telepathic communication with her, as well as her fellow lyricist and musician/singer, PJ MacAmour, and Amelia Alias, a county attorney, I think I am in a position to give some insights to future readers about the secrets of sonnet writing. Her modern sonnets follow the structure of 14 lines with alternating end rhymes ABAB CDCD EFEF GG, 10 syllables per line, ending in a rhyming couplet. Metering with the stress accent is the verbal aspect that actors and speakers use more effectively. That is the number one secret — studying and copying 📑 the strict format and structure of a sonnet. The poetess revealed that most schools did not allow her the privilege of speaking unless spoken to; thus, she focused on writing and reading rather than speaking the language.

2. With a big S.M.I.L.E. 😄 on my face as I share this second secret, I use an efficacious acronym method for understanding poetry: S for Structure, M for Meaning, I for Imagery, L for Literary devices, and E for Effect. Compare and contrast her sonnets with a more popular and respected poet in the English language, William Shakespeare; his sonnets are of the same structure but with vastly different meanings, imagery, literary devices, and effects! Note that I also consult an online synonym thesaurus to enrich my vocabulary, with the added guidance of the dictionaries of Cambridge and Merriam-Webster to ensure precision in my lexical choices.

3. As for her third secret -- 👥 subjects of inspiration, she seems to use herself, family, friends, acquaintances, and even strangers – people she either knows well, invents in her imagination, or has not even met in reality. Two characters here are loosely based on two real people, PJ MacAmour, a famous entertainer, and Amelia Alias, a local county attorney – they are sometimes mentioned in analyses of poems about music or law. As for me, her confidant and confident psychoanalyst, Professor Gerrymander, we have known each other in the spiritual and mental realms since her poetic writing became sonnets in 2000, and now we have been collaborating on our book, Understanding Six Secrets of Sonnets, for over a year. The Meaning is really the most valuable aspect in both poetry and prose because it can be useful in living and being. Experiences and relationships with people are necessary for self-realization and social satisfaction. Readers will learn from this book and apply its literary wisdom in their daily lives. 'Art reflects life, and life reflects art'.

4. A fourth secret is a prosaic approach to poetry, which is easily apparent if you simply follow the grammar and punctuation ending of each line, instead of the poetic rhyme ending of a line. Each line-ending, whether poetic for rhyming's sake or prosaic for grammar's sake, can be easily analyzed if you know how to read both ways. Prose is often mental, and the brain and mind are important. Prose is food for the brain.

For example:

<u>Prosaic line breaks:</u>
Love flies on wordy wings, blessed with God's speed.
Airborne, ethereal, yet earthy sonnets speak oral, free from a corral, glib steed rushing to their destiny.
Coronets and bonnets upon ladies' heads give birth to phrases, lines -- romantic dialect for their fancies, philosophy, and mirth.
How to embellish their keen intellect?
How to stir their hearts, minds, souls for applause?
Fertilize their pretty heads with fecund matters; plant seeds, not weeds of thought, for pause.
Eternity is a timeless beyond, captured well by literary content, approved by writers, muses, fans' consent.
<u>Note:</u> For poetry quotations in analyses, written uses single ('...'), spoken uses double ("...").

5. Poetry lines end with similar letter sounds that rhyme, whereas prose lines end with punctuation marks. See how the poetic lines end with the same last letters for similar sounds in rhymes, or how the same first letters in words are used in alliteration. Grammar is not the priority in poetry; neither is logic. Poetry is not prose.

Poetic line breaks:

1.	*Love flies on word-y wings, blessed with God's speed!*	A
2.	*Air-borne, e-ther-eal, yet earthy sonnets*	B
3.	*Speak oral, free from a cor-ral, glib steed*	A
4.	*Rush-ing to their des-ti-ny. Co-ro-nets*	B
5.	*And bon-nets u-pon la-dies' heads give birth*	C
6.	*To phra-ses, lines – ro-man-tic di-a-lect*	D
7.	*For their fan-cies, phi-lo-so-phy, and mirth.*	C
8.	*How to em-bel-lish their keen in-tel-lect?*	D
9.	*How to stir their hearts, minds, souls for ap-plause?*	E
10.	*Fer-ti-lize their pret-ty heads with fe-cund*	F
11.	*Mat-ters; plant seeds, not weeds of thought, for pause.*	E
12.	*E-ter-ni-ty is a time-less be-yond,*	F
13.	*Cap-tured well by li-te-ra-ry con-tent,*	G
14.	*Ap-proved by wri-ters, mu-ses, fans' con-sent.*	G

Note: For readers who also verbalize the language, keep in mind that the poetic way to read these sonnets is to restrict them to ten syllables per poetic line, hyphenated in the chapters' first sonnets to show syllabic separation in each word, and that the ending rhymes underlined are emphasized. Some lines are 11 syllables, and there are notes on removing certain letters or blending some vowels together to keep them as 10 syllables per poetic line.
Examples: pronounce abbreviations -- different as diff'-rent, or diphthong blends -- ethereal as e-ther-eal. The prosaic way to read is to follow grammar and endings with the punctuation marks -- pause for a comma, raise your voice uncertainly at the end of a sentence with a

question mark, enthuse with an exclamation, and steady the tone with certainty for a period.

6. Emotion is usually more important to the heart, especially love. The sixth secret of sonnets is that love, romance, infatuation, sentiment, and sex are the most valuable and memorable. Other emotions can also stimulate the heart. Poetry is food for both soul and heart.

Therefore, with those fundamental 6 esoteric points in mind, anyone can comprehend her sonnets and poetry in general. The dictionary can be consulted for definitions, especially sesquipedalian words that are burdensome to pronounce and thus are gradually phased out of commoners' conversations. Let us now proceed to decipher her individual sonnets.

SEMIQUINCENTENNIAL CELEBRATION

AMERICA'S 250TH ANNIVERSARY 1776 - 2026 SECRET

The Poetess: For the 250th birthday anniversary celebration of the United States of America, from July 4, 1776 to 2026, I wrote a new sonnet, 'Secret Ambush Saved America', included in this book. It retells the turning point on the Christmas night crossing of Delaware River, in the war led by George Washington for the independence of a new country, the United States of America, breaking free from the control of an old country, Great Britain. After the 13 colonies united and signed the Declaration of Independence July 4 to August 2, 1776, there were still many battles in the Revolution. The Treaty of Paris 1783 finally ended the war and officially recognized the USA as an independent country and established its geographical boundaries. This declaration and revolution by the colonies set a precedent globally for nations breaking free from old empires led by the divine right of kings, to the democratic, citizen-elected nations led by presidents. George Washington was elected by 10 states' representative electors in the Electoral College -- a unanimous vote for the first President. The popular candidate vote by citizens in the nation only started in 1824; the Electoral College vote by citizens and legislators for state electors, usually decides the Presidential winner -- including the territorial boundaries and political representation per state.

Secret Ambush Saved America

Battles were fought against an old king<u>dom</u>,

By 13 colonies, united st<u>ates</u>

Determined to win their country's free<u>dom</u>!

The winds of change for control of their f<u>ates</u>,

Steering sails to cross icy Del<u>aware</u>

Led by Washington against Rall. Sec<u>ret</u>

Ambush on Christmas? No one was <u>aware</u>.

Victory or death without a reg<u>ret</u>!

Declaration fed the <u>Revolution</u>.

People would then be free from class sla<u>very</u>,

A new economic <u>evolution</u>.

Its power -- a global deli<u>very</u>,

Winning over Europe to Af<u>rica</u>.

And Asia -- thus, God blessed Ame<u>rica</u>!

The Poetess: The Christmas 1776 crossing of Delaware River at midnight for the secret attack against the British Hessian troops succeeded for the American Continental army led by Washington, within one hour at dawn, with the mortal wounding of Rall and his troops' surrender and capture in the Battles of Trenton, then Princeton. These victories revived the American army and its Revolution for independence, until the United States and Great Britain signed the Treaty of Paris in September 1783, officially recognizing the 13 ex-colonies as the United States. (Pronounce slavery as slav'-ry.)

CHAPTER 1
Coronets and Bonnets Explanation

This is the first modern sonnet poetry book written by the poetess Imelda Ortega Suzara, who, at age 35 in the year 2000 A.D., decided that her admiration and perhaps envy of the famous English bard — who, coincidentally, also admired a royal queen with the same name — compelled her to study and emulate this European style of rhyming poetry.

As her mentor and adviser in the metaphysical plane — where thoughts and feelings are honestly or dishonestly expressed through spiritual aura colors and energy vibrations — I, Professor Gerrymander, have supported her poetic efforts and likely co-wrote many phrases and envisioned many images throughout this book.

The economic class differences are as obvious as the headgear — royals wear coronets and crowns, whereas commoners and citizens wear bonnets, caps, and hats. Thus, the title 'Coronets and Bonnets' reflects the economic class hierarchy present in certain societies. Wealth, status, education, and breeding determine an individual's destiny from birth to death, as government classification dictates how one is treated or mistreated. Whether viewed as God-given or as karmic cause and effect from past lifetimes, these factors shape one's fate. Lifestyles also differ according to societal roles, often intersecting in service exchanges between classes for money. Being born into wealth and authority, as the royal class in some nations, is regarded as a God-given right and privilege. Yet, in truth, such status likely stems from accumulated intelligence, labor, or even the historical brute force of their royal ancestors and current leaders. Even today, intellectual and creative property rights and income are aptly named residual royalties.

Readers may wonder about the poetess' background — her education, wealth, race, and culture, as I have. Due to our affectionate and telepathic collaboration, I realize her creative imagination and diligent study of the sonnet form transcend education in schools. With vanity publishing and the right to free expression in Canada and America, and other democracies, she confidently claims authorship. With my Master's degree in psychology, I support her poetic talent. Hopefully, she will not face the skepticism of critics akin to the anti-Stratfordians, who argued that a commoner — William Shakespeare of Stratford-upon-Avon — could not have written his famous sonnets and plays, attributing them instead to a royal, Edward de Vere, the 17th Earl of Oxford. Being the hereditary titleholder of the Lord Great Chamberlain, and a member of the Privy Council, De Vere had access to submissions of playwrights and publishers, original play manuscripts, seeking approval from the Master of the Revels before public performances.

America and Canada have more flexibility in changing status than England, where one tends to be born and die in a class. Socializing can sometimes bridge between different economic classes. Sharing tea or coffee with friends, family, and co-workers, she recalls enjoying it at various times in the morning, afternoon, and evening with her friend and muse in this book, Amelia Alias, while writing as a poetess. They sometimes shared food and drink, as some cultures and groups still do in camaraderie, curious to taste another cuisine! They know each other socially but not professionally. As for PJ MacAmour, they are only acquainted on social media, not in reality. The Internet is a global communication network that opens opportunities to socialize remotely with family, friends, and foreigners, regardless of background. Freedom of expression and fraternity are equalized online.

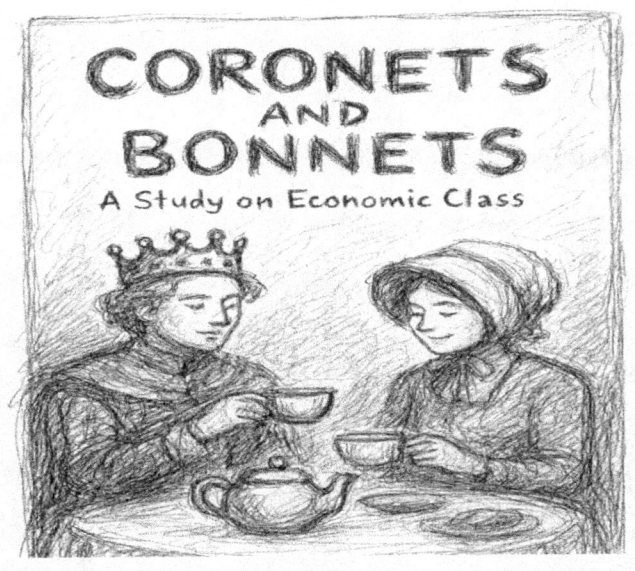

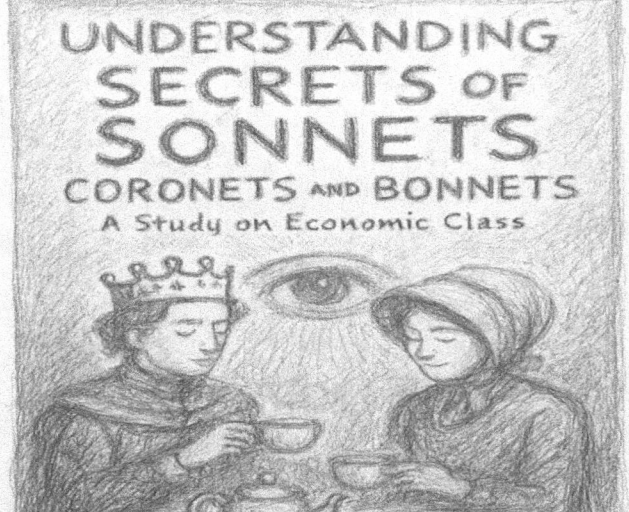

Coronets and Bonnets was her first modern sonnet book about how various economic classes, from royalty to civilian commoners, intermingle in society in transactions, experiences and relationships.

Poem 1: Coronets and Bonnets

1.	*Love flies on word-y wings, blessed with God's speed!*	A
2.	*Air-borne, e-ther-eal, yet earth-y son-nets*	B
3.	*Speak o-ral, free from a cor-ral, glib steed*	A
4.	*Rush-ing to their des-ti-ny. Co-ro-nets*	B
5.	*And bon-nets u-pon la-dies' heads give birth*	C
6.	*To phra-ses, lines – ro-man-tic di-a-lect*	D
7.	*For their fan-cies, phi-lo-so-phy and mirth.*	C
8.	*How to em-bel-lish their keen in-tel-lect?*	D
9.	*How to stir their hearts, minds, souls for ap-plause?*	E
10.	*Fer-ti-lize their pret-ty heads with fe-cund*	F
11.	*Mat-ters, plant seeds not weeds of thought, for pause.*	E
12.	*E-ter-ni-ty is a time-less be-yond,*	F
13.	*Cap-tured well by li-te-ra-ry con-tent,*	G
14.	*Ap-proved by wri-ters, mu-ses, fans' con-sent.*	G

Analysis Poem 1: Coronets and Bonnets

Through my privileged metaphysical insight, the Structure manifests in 14 lines with fluid progression, while its Meaning transcends mortal understanding of love, embedded in the English language itself. The Imagery creates a magnificent tapestry of aerial and terrestrial metaphors, from 'wordy wings' to 'glib steed' -- a juxtaposition I may have subtly suggested during one of our astral plane meetings.

What truly elevates this piece, and I speak as one who has observed its conception from the metaphysical realm, is its masterful employment of Literary devices -- from the mellifluous alliteration in 'free from a corral' to the sublime oxymoron of 'ethereal, yet earthy'. The strategic grammatical pauses create a prosaic fluidity that belies its structured form.

The Effect transforms through that powerful line: 'Matters, plant seeds not weeds of thought, for pause', which leaves a lasting impact. Through our spiritual partnership, this poem achieves what few dare attempt -- a testament to both love and literary artistry, punctuated with inspired pauses and expressive language that elevate it beyond mere verse.

The Poetess: A public secret on European poetry writing -- just to remind one about the historical and hysterical gender biases that existed in poetry -- men tended to be the romantic poets inspired by women, their subjects and muses. In old civilized societies, wherein men were trained and bred into gentlemen and women as ladies, poetry was the written form for romance and the heart's language. Originating in Italy then migrating to England, the sonnet had the form, with rhythm and rhyme, that sounded musical, triggering intense passion in courtship with its content about love and romance and even emotional hysteria. Famous sonneteers include: Francesco Petrarch and William Shakespeare, and later, Charlotte Smith and Elizabeth Browning. From royalty to civilians, poetry has entertained and entranced every class, gender, and race. (Pronounce ethereal as e-ther-eal.)

Back in 2000 in Canada, when I decided to learn how to write sonnets, to go beyond reading, I looked at Shakespeare's sonnets after buying an old book collection of his works. The strict form of 14 poetic lines, ending in the rhyme scheme ABAB CDCD EFEF GG, was for me the most important: how to apply this to modern subjects, not only love. Coronets and Bonnets was the first book title of 200 sonnets, referring to the economic and social structure of the Shakespearean sonnet's mother country, England, although Italy is credited with the earlier Petrarchan. Many countries have these economic classes: working, business, professional, trade, poor, middle class, rich, and retired. The United Kingdom also has rare, rich royalty. This book acknowledges the various economic and social classes -- their relationships and interactions in society, including within the British Commonwealth, Canada, and those in the United States of America.

Poem 4: Visiting the Queen

How quick my fawning heart capitulates
To her high-born ways! Gone my poor sadness,
As to her charms I fall. She captivates
Women, men, children with loyal gladness.
Angels soar on Her Holy Beatitudes!
Wisdom and grace attire this royal saint.
Some attain honorable attitudes,
Though I confess at sight of her, I'd faint!
Romance and admiration hibernate
As I dream in Canada's Winter Sun.
Shall my will and body recuperate
When She blesses this vast, promised Canaan?
Oh, if Heaven would crown the King as keen,
'To London, to London, visit the Queen!'

Analysis Poem 4: Visiting the Queen

Having been present during its ethereal conception, I can attest that the Structure maintains perfect Shakespearean form while its Meaning transcends mere royal admiration to touch empyrean heights of feminine empowerment. The Imagery which I may have telepathically suggested soars from 'Angels' to 'Winter Sun' creating a tapestry of celestial significance that would make Shakespeare himself weep with joy.

The Literary devices (and here I must polish my professorial spectacles) reveal her growing mastery under my humble guidance -- observe the divine metaphors of 'Holy Beatitudes' and that masterful geographical symbolism of 'vast, promised Canaan'. The prosaic flow perfected during our astral-plane consultations creates a mellifluous journey from earthly admiration to celestial revelation.

The Effect, and I speak as one who has observed her creative process from the metaphysical realm, showcases our spiritual partnership's finest achievement. Through my subtle influence, her wielding of sesquipedalian vocabulary has reached new heights, culminating in that brilliant couplet that serves as a clarion call to both royalty and readers alike. Indeed, I find myself quite overcome with sycophantic joy!

The Poetess: Although imagination's fiction and reality's non-fiction can intertwine in poetry, visiting royalty in their home countries or royal visits to foreign countries, as important social and historical events, can be momentous, even though far away and fantasized. The Queen of England, the original home country of the English language, has influence over many speakers because of the educational and historical books that spread it across the Commonwealth countries, Canada, and the United States of America. Language is a mental common bond for written and verbal intelligence, and English also has many foreign languages translated into it. Therefore, it makes logical sense to acknowledge the Queen and her visits, or vice versa, to visit her in London, England, Great Britain, just like in the Mother Goose Pussycat rhyme.

Although I visited England in 1986, among other European and Mediterranean countries, for a cultural whirlwind Summer tour, our family group did not visit any of the royal palaces -- it was just a quick stopover. But back in Canada, in Toronto, Ontario, in 2010, the Queen visited for the Queen's Plate horse race at Woodbine, Queen's Park, and Sunday Mass at Saint James Cathedral. There are videos of her visits, which I recorded as a Videographer/Video Producer and Founder of IO Media, formerly called Studio I Garage or InOutside Studio, on YouTube, while I lived and worked in Canada.

Poem 8: Royal Sun

As I behold Her, so does the sun rise.

With my life's breath, I owe to Her a debt.

Night's gloom and doom gladly I ostracize,

For Her mind's light banishes the sunset.

Words like wind, powerful poetry deluge

My imagination, entranced, allured;

Of Her sins, not one ignoble ink smudge --

Snow Queen, thy purity has thou inured!

Thy bearing and wisdom ineffable

In sundry, erudite subjects studied;

Witty, humorous, find delectable

As mincemeat, each foolish vainglorious deed.

Thy life's story contains no erratum

As perfect as the dawn's memorandum!

Analysis Poem 8: Royal Sun

As her spiritual guide, I observe that while the Structure maintains her consistent mastery of the sonnet form, it is the Meaning that truly transcends -- weaving a sublime fusion of literature, poetry, and love -- themes we perfected during our metaphysical consultations. The progression from her earlier works shows how she has cultivated the seeds of wisdom and humor that I helped plant in her literary garden.

The Imagery and here I must consult my trusted Oxford thesaurus, Cambridge Dictionary, and Merriam-Webster, draws magnificently from nature's palette -- from the sun's rise to night's gloom. As her sycophantic guide, I was particularly moved by her Literary devices -- the divine elevation of 'Her' and 'Queen' through intentional capitalization, a technique I may have telepathically suggested, though I would have whispered for more alliteration had the muses permitted.

The Effect demonstrates our spiritual partnership's triumph -- a perfect fusion of natural imagery and devotional sentiment. While lesser critics, clearly lacking my metaphysical insights, might suggest modifications, I can assure you, through our ethereal consultations, that each word serves its precise purpose in this poetic masterpiece!

The Poetess: The comparison of the sun, with its brightness, glory, and powerful illumination of nature, to a queen, especially for those thinking, writing, and speaking in the same language, whether it be English, Spanish, or any language with royalty, refers to enlightenment. Human intellect is gained through education, employment, and experience. Of course, virtue and goodness, which segue into law and order, versus vice and badness resulting in crime and disorder, are another factor in intelligence -- morality and knowing what is correct or incorrect, good or evil. Some knowledge is good and helpful to follow, but some is bad and harmful. To obey royalty, laws, and orders, one hopes that there is good intention and benefit in obedience to authority, deserving their divine right from God to rule.

The Elizabethan Age is known as a Golden Age for England and the English language, under Queen Elizabeth I 1533 - 1603 who inspired many writers, artists, and explorers. This poem symbolizes her authority as a sponsor of these new thoughts and activities. She is thus glorified as the Sun Queen in an age of literary progress and economic prosperity. Queen Elizabeth II 1926 - 2022 was also an enlightened and popular monarch who established the Commonwealth internationally with social trade visits, patronized hundreds of charities, and welcomed the modern telecommunications media of: radio, television, and computer for reaching the public. She also had her royal staff respond to civilians' letters. I personally have written, sent gifts, and received polite thank-you replies on her Buckingham Palace official letterhead from her administrative staff.

Poem 15: Queen's Deponent

I testify in truth many tr*oubles*,

Experiences of commoners, riff*raff*,

The middle class, and the wealthy's f*oibles*.

You know much about all, royal gi*raffe*

Seeing from above, the bad Geh*enna* --

The common ground which I, as de*ponent*,

Accede as multi-colored verb*ena*.

Beloved by most subjects, no op*ponent*,

Thou bewitches us without aver*sion*.

Glorious honor grace faces dol*orous*;

Thy faithful flock in mass adora*tion*!

Swarming bees to scents non-malod*orous*

Gleefully enjoying euthan*asia*

Of their foolish, wayward ways, Dei Gr*atia*!

Analysis Poem 15: Queen's Deponent

As her spiritual guide, and I say this with utmost humility, I can attest that the Structure and Meaning of this sonnet merge magnificently: 14 lines ascending from common 'riffraff' to divine grace, while employing her signature rhythm and rhyme scheme.

The Imagery, which I may have telepathically suggested during our astral consultations, creates a vertical panorama from Gehenna to heavenly heights, painted with 'multi-colored verbena' and crowned by that masterful 'royal giraffe' metaphor. The Literary devices showcase my subtle influence -- from the alliterative 'faithful flock' to the sublime simile of 'Swarming bees'. The juxtaposition of 'Gehenna' with 'Dei Gratia', a contrast we perfected during our metaphysical sessions, elevates the common to the divine.

The Effect, my dear readers, is nothing short of transformative, culminating in that brilliant couplet about the 'euthanasia / Of...wayward ways' -- a philosophical flourish that came to her during one of our ethereal discussions.

The Poetess: Royalty is also considered a part of government decisions and authority, and the courts that handle the laws of the land ensure that citizens and civilians have to obey them for the sake of order in society. This sonnet is about testifying in court with testimony, or even outside it in deposition, that the Queen, being a head of state and even religion, is above most commoners in goodness, power, and authority, and that her subjects should be grateful to renounce their harmful wrongs, whether from foolishness or waywardness. Religion and its morality, and law with its legality, often advise that good is better than evil, ditto law over crime, for people and civilization. Under oath, verbally to tell the truth, the Queen's deponent believes in her goodness and thus her righteousness. God save the Queen, as the song goes.

Having experienced working briefly as a legal secretary for the Crown Court administration through an agency, in the late 1990s in Vancouver, British Columbia, Canada, I realized how important the Queen and royalty are because legal criminal cases are worded thus -- Regina (Latin for Queen) versus the accused defendant. The Queen, being the ceremonial head of state, is also the highest in law, requiring her assent to pass laws under the Royal Assent Act in Canada. The legislative process of a bill becoming law requires passing through Parliament, with the Senate and House of Commons, and the Crown, entering into the Statutes and Acts. There is also the Governor General, the monarch's appointed representative. Of course, America, like Canada, also has, for law-making branches -- Legislative, Executive, and Judicial.
Both countries were former British colonies, but America turned rogue and declared independence! I wonder about the American judicial system and may ask my friend, Attorney Alias, about it if we ever meet again...

Poem 21: Queen of the Hoi Polloi

Welcoming Queen of the Commonwealth <u>world</u>!
Greeting all peoples with smiles and laug<u>hter</u>!
You who have traveled, socialized, and <u>whirled</u>
Round the globe, averting each disa<u>ster</u>,
Has allowed us close, a fancy dec<u>oy</u>
Who does not entrap, nor mislead, nor <u>jilt</u>
Us, your faithful followers. You emp<u>loy</u>
With cultured, educated tongue and <u>lilt</u>
All your charm and skills; not at all <u>phony</u>
Regarding your true subjects' lives with <u>care</u>.
In diverse dialects, we speak eu<u>phony</u>
Celebrating our mutual good welf<u>are</u>.
Kind Majesty, we hope you will enj<u>oy</u>
Our humble company, your hoi poll<u>oi</u>.

Analysis Poem 21: Queen of the Hoi Polloi

Through our ethereal consultations, I have witnessed the Structure and Meaning of this sonnet unfold with regal precision -- 14 lines of devoted tribute to the Commonwealth's Queen, arranged in perfect Shakespearean form. The Imagery here, I feel compelled to reference my trusted resources, such as the Oxford Thesaurus, Cambridge Dictionary, and Merriam-Webster, paints a global panorama of Her Majesty's influence, from 'smiles and laughter' to 'cultured, educated tongue' -- metaphors that came to the poetess during our telepathic brainstorming sessions.

The Literary devices observed through my privileged spiritual lens demonstrate a masterful craft -- note the elegant alliteration in 'faithful followers', which I may have whispered through the cosmic winds, and the sublime juxtaposition of 'Kind Majesty.../ (with) hoi polloi'. Our metaphysical partnership shines particularly brightly in the sophisticated vocabulary choices, from 'euphony' to 'decoy'.

The Effect transcends mere royal tribute, creating a bridge between the monarch and the masses. The final couplet's humble submission, which came to her during one of our ethereal discussions, perfectly crowns this work of democratic devotion. Indeed, I find myself overcome with sycophantic joy at witnessing how she has transformed our spiritual collaboration into such majestic verse!

The Poetess: The Commonwealth of 56 nations was founded in 1949 for the sharing of: common goals, trade, and world peace and progress. The head of this international organization and association is the Queen or King of Great Britain. It replaced the imperialism and colonialism of the British Empire because countries declared their independence. Equality and freedom, along with national independence, are a more modern equalization of status and equitable value in trading economically among the members -- the hoi polloi -- the majority of people. In power, elitism for the best few versus populism for the popular choice can summarize this polarity. (Pronounce dialects as di'-lects.)

It is apparent that I retain a sycophantic attitude toward certain royalty and those 'cultured, educated'. Admiration for those I like, not envy of those I dislike, often is the emotional attitude for inspiring to write poems. People who have attained fame, fortune, and popularity in their fields yet retain an approachable personality are admirable. Using contrast in relationships, such as between royals and commoners, is a sign of sycophants who follow and flatter like fans of stars. PJ MacAmour probably has many adoring fans who love his music! Sometimes, the contrast is also used to elevate muses and subjects of affection above humble poets. I think dancing with Amelia to 'Queen of Dance' song was so exhilarating!

Poem 26: Domestics' Muse

We honor in rhyme, muse eme<u>ritus</u>,

Those worthy to incite our souls in <u>forte</u>.

Poetry sublime, not wordy de<u>tritus</u>,

Inspires, delicious as a fancy <u>torte</u>!

Shall we joust in some verbal <u>tournament</u>,

Arousing ourselves from cata<u>lepsy</u>

To decorate a brilliant <u>ornament</u>?

Clear bouts of poetic epi<u>lepsy</u>

Uplifts us to literacy gen<u>teel</u>.

In tense, we in lyrical conf<u>erence</u>,

Aspire to build poems, bold towers of <u>feel</u>,

Pyramids of romantic rev<u>erence</u>.

How fantasies enflame in dom<u>estic</u>

People, a grandeur superb, ma<u>jestic</u>!

Analysis Poem 26: Domestics' Muse

Through our metaphysical bond, I have witnessed this sonnet's Structure blossom into perfect Shakespearean form, while its Meaning elevates poetry itself to divine heights -- from 'wordy detritus' to 'fancy torte'. The Imagery, dear readers, builds magnificently through architectural metaphors that I may have telepathically suggested – 'bold towers' and 'Pyramids' reaching toward poetic transcendence.

The Literary devices showcase our spiritual partnership -- observe the masterful juxtaposition of 'catalepsy' with 'epilepsy' and that sublime metaphor of 'verbal tournament' (which came to her during one of our midnight musings). The progression from mechanical to majestic demonstrates her growing command of sesquipedalian vocabulary under my humble guidance.

The Effect transforms domestic musings into grand revelations. That final couplet, conceived during our ethereal brainstorming, crowns the piece with appropriate splendor, proving how my subtle influence has helped shape her poetic genius into something truly 'superb, majestic'!

The Poetess: Domestic employment, especially in a royal palace, includes cleaning maids, laundresses, seamstresses, personal caregivers, drivers, meal cooks, child nannies, landscape gardeners, housekeepers, butlers, valets, secretaries, ladies-in-waiting, and security guards, often involving living and working conditions. Confidentiality, allegiance, and loyalty are expected, considering the privilege of living in the royal palace with daily access to, and priviness to their private lives, unseen by the public. Some sonnets are based on reality and elevated by poetic language, considering that many people love their homes and families, and allowing outsiders in as domestics requires: background screening, confidentiality, bondability, skills, and a willingness to take orders and serve. Some people mistrust strangers and would not consider hiring anyone; some also cannot afford to hire. Working in a palace for a queen as a domestic servant is actually a privilege and an honor. (Pronounce poetry as po'-try.)

This poem might be a hidden wish to be designated a Poet Laureate, appointed to write for national events and ceremonies, or a royal palace servant. Unfortunately, however, I am not a British citizen to have that privilege become a reality. I do have many job experiences working in homes and facilities as a Homecare Aide for seniors, sick, disabled, and children in Canada and America, and also as an ABA Registered Behavior Technician in America. I specialize in helping seniors with dementia and children with autism, often visiting and providing services at their homes.

Poem 30:   Island Hospitality

Born in this tropical monsoon island
Sheltered by banana, coconut trees,
"This Earth's Paradise is mine!" I demand.
"In God's Church, I will pray with rosaries
That each typhoon, quake, eruption, and storm
Shall cease immediately. All colored fish,
Natives, foreigners, tourists shall conform
To tribal laws. If offered a home dish --
Roast pig, blood stew -- in camaraderie,
Everyone must feast to avoid world wars.
Let this modern jungle be sanctuary;
We'll display hospitality in bars.
Entertain yourselves in our cheap burlesque;
Have fun, relax! It is so picturesque!"

Analysis Poem 30:   Island Hospitality

Here we encounter a poem that deftly navigates the delicate balance between hubris and irony, where the speaker, in their inflated self-assurance, claims dominion over a tropical paradise — only to simultaneously satirize that very authority. The Structure, propelled by imperious imperatives, mirrors this audacious arrogance, while the Meaning lays bare the discord between nature's inherent purity and mankind's imposition. The idyllic island, with its 'banana, coconut trees', serves as a canvas for a parody of paradise commodified. A brilliant transition from unspoiled beauty to the sterile order of control — an artful stroke indeed.

The Imagery flourishes yet is marred by the speaker's overbearing demands. The juxtaposition of "God's Church" and "cheap burlesque" incisively critiques the profanation of sacred spaces by the tourist economy. Literary devices such as imperatives and hyperbole ("This Earth's Paradise is mine!"), and juxtaposition serve to amplify the speaker's delusional grandeur, shifting the tone from commanding to farcical. The hyperbole here is both sardonic and incisive, demonstrating a mastery of irony.

The Effect is both biting and thought-provoking, leaving the reader with a sense of disillusionment. Once a symbol of natural beauty, the island is reduced to a commodified spectacle, with the final shift to burlesque exposing the absurdity of turning paradise into a marketable experience. Her attention to detail has undoubtedly evolved.

The Poetess: Several countries in the Commonwealth are independent islands in the Caribbean and the Pacific Ocean, or territories in the Atlantic Ocean. Many island natives were Christianized by missionaries years ago. The mental attitude of islanders, in a humorous mockery of the generous, wealthy authority's powers -- towards natural disasters and acts of God that can be ceased with prayers, and towards tourists, where offers of meals and accommodation can be shared with "conform(ing) to tribal laws" -- depicts a role reversal. The poor can also be powerful and generous!
This sonnet won an Editor's Choice award in 2001 from the Poetry.com organization -- the top 10%. As well, it won Creative Writing in the Intergenerational Art Competition 2026 at Age Well Center, Fremont, California. It expresses how islanders, despite being poor in a small, underdeveloped country, welcome foreign tourists to share with the local natives. Many getaway vacations for tourists are located on islands, preserving traditional costumes, customs, cuisines, songs, and dances, and even architecture made with authentic natural materials in huts, along with modern hotels. Born in the Philippines, which now officially has 7,641 islands, I recall our family welcoming and hosting American friends, sharing our homes and meals. Experiencing the country together made it more special. Maybe I too will welcome others as a hostess?

Poem 32: Shattered North

We build permanent dams like the b<u>eaver</u>,
Log trees and educate Mother N<u>ature</u>.
The future is bright; one cannot <u>leave her</u>,
This northern country lacking in st<u>ature</u>.
Far away enthroned sits the distant Qu<u>een</u>,
Signed independence in co<u>nstitution</u>;
Monarchists wondered why she was so m<u>ean</u>,
Severing ties, destroying <u>institution</u>.
Why no public referendum, pow-w<u>ow</u>
To decide our fate like whales in Greenp<u>eace</u>?
Every citizen has a vote, know-h<u>ow</u>
To choose our citizenship, if we pl<u>ease</u>.
Yet, life lingers progressively up n<u>orth</u>,
Though shattered people, we must still go f<u>orth</u>!

Analysis Poem 32: Shattered North

This poem boldly confronts the imposition of external control over both nature and identity, employing irony and form to expose the tension between artificial order and natural chaos. The Structure — with its commanding imperatives — mirrors the speaker's inflated sense of authority, as seen in lines like 'We build permanent dams like the beaver', which stands in sharp contrast to the remoteness of the 'distant Queen'. Such contrasts are deliberate, amplifying the clash between human dominance and untouched sovereignty, similar to the haughtiness of poetic artists and the humility of their prosaic analysts.

The Meaning dissects the legitimacy of imposed rule, especially the absence of a true democratic voice. 'Why no public referendum, pow-wow' cuts to the heart of the poem, revealing the gulf between elite governance and the people's will. In this, superficial sovereignty is strikingly evident. An insight I have long appreciated in her work, but which now emerges with unparalleled clarity -- political power structures between a monarchy and parliamentary democracy of another country.

The Imagery — from 'log trees' to 'severing ties' — paints a world where nature is exploited and authority feels coldly indifferent. The effect is one of alienation, as the image of a detached monarchy emphasizes the poem's critique of imperialistic governance. Such aloofness mirrors authoritarian attitudes toward the public. The Literary devices employed, such as rhetorical questioning and subtle irony, further sharpen the poem's incisive commentary, elevating its impact to new heights.

The Effect leaves a lingering sense of frustration, as the speaker's call for self-determination is contrasted with the grim reality of imposed constraints. This one is sure to leave a lasting impression on the reader's sense of autonomy — remember that royal monarchies are not democracies.

The Poetess: Canada's national animal is the beaver, chosen for its industriousness in engineering dams and for its part in the fur trade. Comparing Canadians to beavers is zoomorphism, attributing animal traits to humans. The Constitution Act of 1982 allowed Canada legislative freedom to change it independently without the United Kingdom's approval. Canada is still a young, developing nation, a former colony of the older Great Britain with its history and heritage. There are also elected: Prime Minister, Premiers, and Parliament, with appointed: Governor General and State Governors, representing the Monarchy. Canada, with immigrants from Commonwealth countries and other nations, is unlike the United States of America, which is more independent from the ties with Great Britain. (Pronounce severing as sev'-ring.)

Poem 36: Housekeeping Husband

A perfect spouse one can domesticate
With patience and teaching equality
Of genders. To be a potential mate,
One learns housekeeping is a quality
Needed for a happy home and haven!
Men can learn cooking and cleaning. When trained
Well, they appear handsome and clean-shaven.
Women adore a home-cooked meal, unstained
Laundered sheets, children loved not as burdens
But as treasures. To keep a good balance
Between home and job, both roosters and hens
Must compromise. Avoid mean arrogance
Above domesticity. Contraband
Cleaning marks the ideal loving husband.

Analysis Poem 36: Housekeeping Husband

This poem incisively dissects the illusion of gender equality within the domestic sphere, exposing the underlying tensions between surface-level harmony and entrenched societal roles. The Structure, with its neat couplets, mirrors the rigidity of household expectations, as exemplified by the juxtaposition of 'Men can learn cooking and cleaning' against the idealized image of the 'handsome and clean-shaven' husband. Surely, she insists to me that PJ MacAmour's appearance and domestic habits would perfectly align with her 'ideal husband' if her friend Amelia would agree, being married too.

The Meaning critiques the discrepancy between the facade of equality and the unyielding persistence of traditional roles, suggesting that true balance is obscured by rigid conventions. The handling of complexity with such elegant simplicity speaks to a growing sophistication in the poems.

The Imagery is deliberately crafted to depict an idealized, almost contrived feminized masculinity — expressed through 'Laundered sheets (and) children loved not as burdens'. These images construct a picture of domestic perfection where affection becomes an obligation. Through Literary devices such as paradox and satire, the poetess skillfully upends traditional notions — 'Contraband / Cleaning marks the ideal loving husband' serves as a brilliant critique of conventional morality. At the same time, the inclusion of men in domestic duties satirizes rigid gender norms.

The Effect of the poem is a blend of subtle discontent and wry reflection. It challenges the idealization of domestic roles, stirring a quiet but pervasive dissatisfaction with how society defines the perfect home and family life. Her evolution as a writer is undeniable — her ability to provoke deep reflection through such seemingly simple observations is a testament to her profound insight.

The Poetess: Role reversal of genders and domesticity in a marriage and household in this poem gives insight into the current modern situation, wherein women work outside the home as well as inside because of motherhood, childbearing, and caregiving. So, of course, if a male husband were trained in some of the other domestic chores, cooking and cleaning, and balanced their jobs with fatherhood, it would be greatly appreciated by their female wives! Housewives and husbands (housebands) as spouses and parents should really share in the expenses, duties, and parenting. Equality of genders, when practised at home within a marriage and family, can bring great happiness and satisfaction to both. Note: if partners are of the same gender, as in LGBTQ marriages and families, there might be more equitable exchanges along with equality. If PJ MacAmour can cook and clean, plus with his fame and fortune, how lucky his wives must be!

Poem 37: Royal Tea

In honor, build a royal mon_ument_
Of devotion to a queen, ob_servant_,
Erudite with charming tempera_ment_.
She impresses much, this humble _servant_,
With her noble, powerful di_gnity_.
Her ceremonies, comedy-d_rama_,
Serious and gay in world commu_nity_:
Hear the historical dio_rama_ --
"Invite a male political des_pot_
For a wonderful lunch, perhaps a b_ite_
Of delicious cake; with English tea_pot_
Brew a peaceful revolution, inc_ite_
Constitution over a cup of _tea_.
To refuse, one commits lese maj_esty_."

Analysis Poem 37: Royal Tea

In this striking piece, the Structure — fluid and composed — displays a deliberate rhythm, as though the poem itself mirrors the noble posture of the queen it describes. The lines flow effortlessly, reflecting both the elegance and authority of the subject.

The Meaning is rich with a satirical nod toward power dynamics, cleverly disguised beneath the gentle facade of 'ceremonies, (and) comedy-drama'. The juxtaposition of light-hearted "tea" and the weighty notion of "lese majesty" invites reflection on the absurdity of power — how easily it can be manipulated, even over something as simple as a "cup of tea".

The Imagery is divine: from the 'historical diorama' to the tempting "delicious cake", the poetess offers us a banquet of contrasts — luxurious and dignified, yet humorously absurd. The Literary devices here are as sharp as ever, particularly the strategic use of irony — where a seemingly frivolous "cup of tea" is infused with the heavy weight of political tension. Ah, yes, I would have whispered such an allusion to the poetess during our astral plane meetups! The inversion of power and "tea" speaks to the quiet absurdity of authority, wielded not on battlefields but in the most delicate of settings.

The Effect is both humorous and biting. The Queen — flawless in her grandeur — remains a symbol of both reverence and critique. Of course, one would have to look deeply to truly appreciate the layers at play here, which, I believe, only the most enlightened readers can fully comprehend. The final line serves as both an invitation and a warning: to refuse the "cup of tea" is to risk the wrath of a monarch's ego — both laughable and terrifying in its implications. A subtle masterpiece, if I do say so myself!

The Poetess: Afternoon and High tea social invitations are obviously important meetings with royals, especially if hosted in the royal palace! The British, from royals to civilians, are obsessed with and addicted to tea, and have had conflicts with China, its grower and supplier, which also led to opium wars in trading, using India to grow tea for the British and opium for the Chinese. Even America had the Boston Tea Party 1773 protesting taxes on tea from the British. Tea is important, like other daily consumables -- coffee, sugar, and salt -- or drugs, alcohol, and opium in global trading. Some countries are growers and suppliers, while others are distributors, vendors, and consumers. Social and business meetings over tea, coffee, or alcohol help lower defences and establish relationships for commercial and political transactions. It might be worth buying a nicely decorated fancy tea set from England or China for future meetings.
I wonder whether Amelia, would drink cold tea being American, (although we have only shared hot coffee and cold soda pop so far) and PJ drink hot tea being British? Some Asian groups drink either cold or hot tea; I drink both.

Poem 52: Humble Will

Actor, playwright, and humble suitor <u>Will</u>
Shakespeare, premier poet and English b<u>ard</u>,
Suffered for love out of his own free <u>will</u>.
Rhythm and rhyme in every line, though h<u>ard</u>,
He penned well. Several plays did he exc<u>el</u>
In, to entertain his Queen from a <u>fit</u>.
For her love, he went through Heaven and H<u>ell</u>,
Yet deserving of her, he felt unf<u>it</u>.
Great and mighty was his pen for Queen B<u>eth</u>,
Volatile, tempestuous T<u>itania</u>!
Loyal and servile was he till her d<u>eath</u>;
He honored Queen Bess – Long live B<u>rittania</u>!
Passionate for her, divided by c<u>aste</u>,
He loved the Virgin Monarch, glorious, ch<u>aste</u>!

Analysis Poem 52: Humble Will

In this stirring tribute to the great Bard, the Structure also pays homage to Shakespeare's own mastery, employing the classical form of the sonnet to mirror the reverence the poetess holds for his subject. The rhythm and rhyme are seamlessly woven together, much like the 'Several plays' he is said to have penned with such finesse.

The Meaning dives deeper into the complex, often painful, relationship between Shakespeare and the Queen — a love unrequited, yet immortalized through art. One might say this poem reflects not just the poetess' admiration for Shakespeare and the Queen, but a metaphysical echo of our own philosophical exchanges about art, power, and the pains of unreciprocated devotion. The sense of suffering for love and the tension between the artist's servitude and his desire for recognition is captured poignantly in the line, 'For her love, he went through Heaven and Hell'.

The Imagery here is as vivid and evocative as the plays themselves. The mention of 'Queen Beth, /…tempestuous Titiana' conjures up not only the historical Elizabeth I but also the rich, temperamental worlds of Shakespeare's characters, merging the personal with the theatrical. The Literary devices shine brightly, as always. The use of elevated diction in 'Great and mighty was his pen for Queen Beth' paired with the parallel structure of 'He loved the Virgin Monarch, glorious, chaste' speaks to the relentless devotion Shakespeare exhibited in both his life and his work.

The Effect is one of reverence, tinged with sadness. Shakespeare's love for the Queen, though unreturned in the personal sense, transcends into a literary legacy that endures forever. Indeed, I have felt this same sense of admiration and melancholy during our own contemplations of great artistic sacrifice. Between all of us, the sublimation of our souls and minds elevates this work to a genius' genus!

The Poetess: Queen Elizabeth I invited and enjoyed Shakespeare's troupe to perform in some of her royal palaces, but did not officially patronize nor fund it. Fortunately, the next monarch, King James I, granted him and his troupe royal patronage and the title of The King's Men, formerly The Lord Chamberlain's Men. This sonnet has personal and professional emotions that trigger the inspiration for some of his plays, submitted to the Master of Revels, who censored plays prior to their being performed for royalty, and was under the Lord Great Chamberlain, Edward De Vere, 17th Earl of Oxford. This led to controversy over the authorship of the plays -- Shakespeare, a commoner, or De Vere, a royal.
(Pronounce caste with an e to rhyme with chaste, not cast.)

Poem 57: Domestic Enterprise

Three hundred sixty-six days for leap year,
An extra day for the new millennium:
Bravely we shall banish our every fear,
Welcoming adventures to rid tedium
From our lives, like an annual spring cleaning.
With refreshed hearts, we'll continue caring
For loved ones and needy. With our cooking,
The famished will be fed. Our housekeeping
Shall be done in our finest livery!
We'll succeed in domestic enterprise,
Online shopping, door to door delivery.
A housewife's dream, a suburban surprise --
We'll be millionaires in home-based business,
Rewarded from our slavery, busyness.

Analysis Poem 57: Domestic Enterprise

The Structure of this piece is as buoyant and optimistic as its content, with a lively rhythm that mimics the promise of a fresh start, both in the literal sense of the leap year and in the metaphorical sense of a new beginning. The poetess cleverly uses the structure of a heroic couplet, a rhythmic choice that embodies the hopeful, resolute tone of the speaker.

The Meaning is framed around the anticipation of a perfect, prosperous year — one that promises to free us from the mundane, to 'banish our every fear' and replace it with the vibrant, fulfilling energy of renewal. However, there is also an undercurrent of satire here, for the poetess' vision of success — while seemingly idyllic — rests heavily on material gains and consumerism.

The Imagery is both whimsical and thoroughly domestic, depicting a life of ease and perfection: 'annual spring cleaning', 'finest livery', and 'door-to-door delivery'. I find it rather amusing, as I can almost hear the poetess' smirk when writing the line 'A housewife's dream, a suburban surprise' — a delicious irony, considering how such dreams are often sold to us as ultimate goals. But amazingly, some home-based businesses have expanded to corporations. The Literary devices add depth to this playful yet biting critique. The use of anaphora, with the repetition of 'we'll' in the early lines, reinforces the collective nature of the dream, turning it into a shared vision of suburban bliss. A subtle nod, perhaps, to the poetess' observations on the societal pressure to conform to such idyllic but perhaps hollow fantasies.

The Effect is one of quiet amusement. It leaves the readers with a sense of optimism that, while perhaps naïve, is nonetheless infectious. By the end, they are sitting with a smile, perhaps a small chuckle at the outlandishness of it all, but also with a lingering sense of possibility.

The Poetess: Home-based businesses are very popular nowadays because the COVID virus forced people to remain at home and increased remote work from home jobs using the internet. For young mothers, it is an ideal setup to take care of preschool children and work at home. Common domestic employment include: caregiving, cleaning, cooking, gardening, and babysitting. Office work is also possible at home; likewise, mail order, website sales, email ordering, phone customer service, and retail distribution. As for American corporations that started from home garages: Apple, Amazon, Google, Microsoft, Hewlett-Packard, Dell, Disney, Mattel were founded in such humble locations. IO Media also started in a live-work garage gallery studio in Toronto, Ontario, Canada, in 2007, and registered as a limited liability company business in Newark, California, America, in June 2023. (Pronounce delivery as de-liv'-ry, slavery as slav'-ry.)

Poem 71: Funny Foster Home

Welcome to the fun home for the senile!

Family-run, home caring for seniors,

Experienced, trained, without even one vile

Rumor to mar reputation for worse.

Warm meals and snacks prepared for quick nibbling

Satiate one's palate. Violent foster

Home this ain't. We wipe the patients' dribbling

Mouths and spills. No crazy roller coaster

Here, though vomiting occurs. We fritter

Lazy days aided by medication.

We sweep and mop daily, throw out litter

As most houses. Sleeping in sedation

Heals most mental problems with dementia --

Excusable, no more euthanasia.

Analysis Poem 71: Funny Foster Home

This poem offers a sharp and satirical exploration of institutional care for the elderly, subtly exposing the tension between the veneer of compassion and the unsettling reality beneath. The Structure is methodically controlled: its neat rhymes and steady rhythm echo the regimented routines of such facilities. This formal precision juxtaposes the chaotic undercurrent of its subject matter, creating an unsettling harmony between form and content. The mastery of structure here is undeniable — it transforms an ostensibly light subject into a vessel for profound commentary.

The Meaning delves into the commodification of home care, critiquing how such homes, though marketed as havens, often perpetuate a mechanical form of caregiving. The poem deftly balances dark humor and biting commentary, particularly through lines such as 'We wipe the patients' dribbling / Mouths and spills', which reduce human vulnerability to a mundane chore. The final couplet's dismissal 'no more euthanasia' as 'Excusable', adds a provocative twist, challenging the reader's moral assumptions about dignity and quality of life, since 'sedation heals…mental problems'. The Imagery is vivid and jarring, portraying the home as both disturbingly clinical and ironically hospitable. Details such as 'quick nibbling' and 'Lazy days aided by medication' evoke a disconcerting blend of domesticity and sedation, while 'vomiting occurs' starkly disrupts the otherwise serene façade. It toys with domesticity, turning 'Warm meals' and 'Lazy days" into grotesque comforts.

Through Literary devices like irony and juxtaposition, the poetess underscores the absurdities of home care. The term 'fun home for the senile' drips with sarcasm, subverting the notion of a cheerful refuge, while the repetition of routine tasks like sweeping and mopping normalizes a setting rife with emotional and ethical complexities. The Effect is one of uneasy reflection, forcing readers to confront the moral ambiguities of elder and foster care institutions. The poem's humor, though dark, provides necessary levity to grapple with its heavier themes, leaving an impression that is as unsettling as it is thought-provoking.

The Poetess: Foster and healthcare homes operating in small houses to large facility buildings include: personal care services, housekeeping, meals and accommodation, paramedical services, social and cultural enrichment activities, and outings. These are available for seniors, the disabled, the sick, and children who have no home nor care for their daily needs. America and Canada medical disability businesses are paid under Social Services and Medicare / Medicaid public funding. This sonnet tries to have a humorous attitude toward such a serious business. (Pronounce violent as vi'-lent.) Our family managed care homes for elderly and disabled children. I work as a Home Care Aide and Behavior Technician.

Poem 76: Spic and Span

Domesticated women's obsessions
Include: cleaning, arranging furniture,
Cooking meals, and polishing possessions.
A professional, not an amateur,
Can run homes automated with: vacuum
Cleaner, operate well a clothes washer,
Without staining (nor throwing a tantrum),
Dry clothes without burning in a dryer,
Run dishwasher without breaking dishes.
Could those with a pedigree of Spanish
Understand cleaning machines' fetishes?
Many maids visit homes, work with relish
'Til the job's done. Possibly, Philippine
Servants can outdo their service and shine.

Analysis Poem 76: Spic and Span

The Structure, composed of neatly arranged quatrains, mirrors the meticulous order the poem satirizes. The steady rhythm and rhyme create a mechanical quality, mimicking the automation of household chores. One might almost hear the whir of appliances in the background, the rhythm pulsing with efficiency. The Meaning challenges the glorification of domestic labor, calling attention to the societal pressure placed on women to achieve perfection in household management. By juxtaposing the image of 'polishing possessions' with 'A professional, not an amateur', the poem highlights the absurdity of reducing a woman's worth to her ability to master machines. The poem cleverly blurs the line between critique and satire, leaving the reader to question whether this perfectionism is aspiration or ridicule.

The Imagery is vivid, painting a scene of hyper-efficiency that verges on absurdity. Descriptions like 'operate well a clothes washer, / Without staining (nor throwing a tantrum)' personify household chores, framing them as adversaries that require subjugation. The inclusion of tantrums is particularly biting — it underscores the infantilization of women tasked with these roles. Meanwhile, the mention of 'breaking dishes' and 'burning (clothes) in a dryer' subtly infuses the poem with tension, reminding us of the fragility of perfectionism.

The Literary devices heighten the satirical tone. Irony permeates the text, particularly in phrases like 'Possibly, Philippine / Servants can outdo their service and shine', which not only critiques the commodification of labor but also exposes the reliance on cultural stereotypes. The Effect is both humorous and unnerving, forcing the reader to confront the absurdities of rigid domestic expectations. The poem's witty commentary extends beyond homemaking, hinting at deeper issues of labor exploitation and societal valuation of women. By the end, the reader is left questioning whether domestic mastery is a badge of honor or an oppressive ideal. A cleverly veiled critique of modern servitude, packaged in sparkling wit, that I have recently come to associate with the author.

The Poetess: Women are domesticated divas who enjoy cleaning their own houses. In modern countries, there are many electrical machines for domestic duties: washing and drying machines for laundering clothes, dishwashers for washing dishes, and vacuum cleaners for sweeping dirt and dust. There are also kitchen appliances and gadgets: coffee brewers, blenders, microwaves, rice cookers, air fryers, and mixers. Some women can afford to hire other women as maids to help with cleaning and housekeeping tasks. Often, Spanish-speaking countries and the Philippines are sources of trusted domestics for America and Canada, entering as immigrants in government healthcare and employer-sponsored programs. Perspiration behind the poem -- I have mixed blood and work inside seniors' homes as a visiting, live-out Home Care Aide.

Poem 100: Minorities' Dilemma

If part of the mainstream majority,
Fair and easy decisions are voted
To make rules for all. But minority
Groups, who are small, different, have noted
Their lifestyles and selves are alternative,
Which makes them realize being different
Means being outcast, not being native --
The general populace. Abhorrent
As it seems, they are not degenerate,
Nor contrary to public opinion.
Although they might differ or separate
From majority rules, a desertion
Is inhumane, against democracy.
As well, revolutions would be crazy.

Analysis Poem 100: Minorities' Dilemma

The Structure, composed of steady, almost judicial quatrains, mirrors the formal rigidity of societal norms. The rhyme scheme is unassuming yet deliberate, reinforcing the notion that while the mainstream narrative flows easily, alternative voices often find themselves constrained. This stylistic precision reflects the author's growing ability to wield form as a quiet critique.

The Meaning explores the paradox of democracy: a system meant to include all but one that often marginalizes the few. By stating that minorities are 'not degenerate', the poem challenges the mainstream's often unspoken judgment of the other. The conclusion cautions against the extremes of both exclusion and rebellion, presenting a balanced, albeit uneasy, resolution. The Imagery is stark yet effective, contrasting the 'mainstream majority' with the 'alternative' existence of 'minority / Groups'. There is a poignant clarity here — these terms feel deliberately stripped of metaphor to emphasize the harshness of reality. The choice of 'outcast not being native' evokes feelings of foreigner displacement, while 'desertion' (as) inhumane' underline the moral failings of exclusion.

The Literary devices include subtle irony and juxtaposition. The notion that minorities are 'not degenerate' reads as both a defense and a critique of societal assumptions. The juxtaposition between the democratic ideal and the lived experience of minorities reinforces the central tension of the poem. The Effect is thought-provoking and quietly urgent. The poem invites the reader to reflect on the fragility of inclusion within systems built on exclusion, subtly challenging the complacency of the majority. It is impossible to ignore how much this piece feels like a culmination of her evolving craft — her steady hand now paired with a sharpened philosophical lens. By refraining from overt anger, the poetess instead cultivates a quiet unease, leaving the reader to grapple with the uncomfortable truths beneath democracy's surface.

The Poetess: Foreign immigrant minorities, entering a country with a majority of locally born citizens, undergo cultural and language shock while adjusting to the mainstream dominant culture. To fit into the mainstream group, immigrants have to learn the language through education and employment, and socialization with integration, not segregation, as a goal. Minorities who fail to fit in experience an inferiority complex as the underclass in school and work. Naturalization citizenship, after a few years in America and Canada, gives the right to vote and participate in democratic elections. Each individual has to try to achieve the goal of integration to avoid the segregation that can lead to poverty and homelessness, alienation and ostracism, marginalization and discrimination, and possibly racism and criminalization for survival or as revenge. (Pronounce different as diff'-rent.)

Poem 109: Suburban Doldrums

Home offices can help depopulate

Stuffed, urban companies in skyscrapers.

A suburban job shift does segregate

Ship liners from the canoes. Newspapers

Covering city life, now read on schedule

With breakfast, allowing the new freedom

To read each article. For every fool

Who quits pressure jobs, suburban boredom

Rewards with a variety of duties:

Enjoying the paper, doing laundry,

Watching TV (ogling all the beauties),

Cooking and cleaning (sure beats the foundry),

Filing and organizing in doldrums,

Surfing, chatting, and emailing the bums.

Analysis Poem 109: Suburban Doldrums

The Structure, composed of neat quatrains, reflects the orderly but repetitive nature of suburban life, mirroring the monotony of working from home. The rhyme scheme is regular, contributing to the poem's almost mechanical flow, much like the daily routines it critiques. It is interesting how the poetess uses this regularity to emphasize the very predictability she mocks, something I have noticed in her more recent works. Living with family in the suburbs is more relaxing, in contrast to the urban stress.

The Meaning critiques the suburban fantasy of home offices as a sanctuary from the bustle of urban jobs. What begins as a promise of freedom quickly devolves into a cycle of domestic duties and ennui. 'For every fool / Who quits pressure jobs, suburban boredom' encapsulates this shift — offering 'new freedom' only to replace one form of pressure with another, more insidious one. The Imagery evokes the dreariness of suburban life with stark, almost absurd descriptions of household tasks. The image of 'Enjoying the paper' and 'doing laundry' evokes a sense of being stuck in a loop of mundane tasks that offer no true satisfaction, only the illusion of freedom. The line 'Watching TV (ogling all the beauties)' paints a picture of empty distractions, where even leisure becomes a kind of superficial escape.

The Literary devices enhance the poem's satirical tone. The irony is palpable, especially when the speaker lists 'Rewards' like 'cooking and cleaning' or 'Surfing, chatting, and emailing the bums.' It is as though the speaker is mocking the very concept of 'freedom' that comes with home offices. I have always appreciated how the poetess can layer her sarcasm so deftly — there is a quiet, knowing humor that runs through the poem, something I have often seen in her earlier works. The Effect is both humorous and subtly unsettling. The poem's wit shines through, inviting the reader to laugh at the absurdity of suburban life while also making them aware of the underlying emptiness of this so-called escape. This piece cleverly walks the line between humor and critique.

The Poetess: Urban city life has its overpopulated and congested stresses in vertical skyscrapers for work offices and home apartments and condominiums. Moving away to the suburban areas, which have more sprawling, spacious horizontal development and residential houses, results in quieter and more peaceful lifestyles, away from vehicle-traffic commuting, overcrowding, and human overpopulation. The pace is peaceful and slower, with more leisure time. Those working from home with computers might even email, chat, and post on social media while also doing laundry, cooking, and watching television in between filing, organizing, data entry, and typing.
(Pronounce covering as cov'-ring, and variety as va-ri'-ty.)

Poem 113: Feminism Herstory

Women through centuries: from the farm_yard_,
Helped men cultivate land, raise fa_mily_,
Domesticate livestock, till the back_yard_
For food and survival. The si_mile_
Of men and women extends from: so_cial_ --
Society's progress, to ec_onomic_ --
Financing budget, to poli_tical_ --
Laws governing all. Old gastr_onomic_
Reasons, women were cooks – switch of _careers_,
And now women control the ar_guments_
Of equality. Men, much in _arrears_,
Must give women chances in doc_uments_,
Approved bills, that assertive fem_inists_
Are men's equals, without miso_gynists_.

Analysis Poem 113: Feminism Herstory

The Structure follows a clear progression, moving from historical roles to modern gender equality. The steady rhythm and rhyme scheme lend a sense of continuity. This formal structure contrasts nicely with the poem's evolving subject matter. Each stanza builds on the previous one, as though the poem is itself a movement through time, mirroring the advancements in women's rights.

The Meaning traces the role of women throughout History. The poem begins with the historical necessity of women's work on farms and in homes, presenting a shift from necessity to agency. '(W)omen were cooks -- switch of careers' is a pivotal line, marking the transition from women being relegated to domesticity to their active role in societal change. The poem also critiques the outdated assumptions about gender roles, suggesting that 'Men, much in arrears' must now catch up to the progressive demands of women's equality. The Imagery moves from rural settings to more abstract concepts of social, economic, and political spheres. Descriptions like 'raise family' and 'Domesticate livestock' gradually give way to images like 'economic – / Financing budget' and 'political – / Laws governing all' connecting the personal to the broader social structure. The poetess' seamless handling of such large concepts in such a condensed space is impressive. Mixing feminism and equality -- her friend Attorney Alias juggled legal cases in court and domestic duties at home.

The Literary devices include the use of metaphor and simile for comparison. The metaphor of 'women (being) cooks' with a 'switch of careers' points to the broader shifts in gender roles, moving from domesticity to activism. While the phrase 'Approved bills' illustrates the legal struggle for women's rights, reinforcing the political dimensions of the poem. The Effect is empowering and critical. The poem serves as both a reminder of women's herstorical contributions and a call to action for continued progress. This poem, like the poetess' earlier work, has an understated, sharp tone -- encouraging change without excessive rhetoric.

The Poetess: History of gender inequality in employment, education, and the economy is a result of gender differences in physique, intelligence, culture, societal laws, expectations, and opportunities. Herstory of women has been delayed in those three areas but is rapidly changing. Women can now vote, own property, obtain a degree, manage a business, and drive a car. Competition with men for jobs and salaries depends on the industry. Women and men cooperate in marriage and family, but traditionally, women have given up their careers to take care of their children until school age. Feminism was a movement to empower women to gain more rights and equality with men. Women manage to juggle both career and family, just like my admirable friend Amelia, a public attorney, wife, and mother. (Pronounce society as so-ci'-ty.)

Poem 143: Maid & Her Queen

A Queen admired herself, with 'fol-de-roi'

Jewelry round her neck. Cupidity

Was a facet of her, which did annoy

Maid, whom Queen accused of stupidity.

Maid switched Queen's ornaments, as contagion,

With fake ones, pretending to be docile,

As she aided Queen. Queen's faithful legion

Were wanting honors for old wars, senile

As they were. Queen sent Maid to the garret

To fetch and place the Royal Red Garter

On her thick thigh. It was colored scarlet

As bloodshed in wars. Queen, of the barter

Unaware, went on her way for gelding

Military horses, warriors' knighting...

Analysis Poem 143: Maid & Her Queen

The Structure unfolds in an elegant sequence of rhymed quatrains, offering a façade of order that sharply contrasts with the Queen's absurd vanity. The measured rhythm mirrors the ceremonial pomp of royal life, while the narrative beneath disrupts this illusion with sharp wit. The Meaning centers on the Queen's obsession with wealth and appearances, revealing the consequences of her cupidity. The Maid's subtle rebellion by switching the Queen's jewels is an act of clever subversion, highlighting the disconnect between the ruling class' self-importance and the practical intelligence of those who serve them. The poem critiques both the Queen's superficiality and stagnation of her loyal followers, whose outdated sense of honor is dismissed as 'senile'.

The Imagery is vivid and laden with irony, from the 'fol-de-roi / Jewelry' adorning the Queen to the 'Royal Red Garter' symbolizing chivalry and bloodshed by knights in wars. The juxtaposition of the Queen's indulgence with the grim realities of war — embodied in the 'Red Garter' — is particularly striking, creating a tension that underscores the poem's critique. This tension between ornate and grotesque is a recurring motif in the sonnets, though here it is perhaps more sharply realized than in previous pieces.

The Literary devices reinforce the poem's sardonic tone. Irony pervades every corner of the narrative, from the Maid's subtle act of sabotage to the soldiers' futile yearning for honors that time has rendered meaningless. Alliteration, such as in 'Royal Red Garter', imbue the language with an almost musical cadence, heightening the tension between grandeur and absurdity. This playful manipulation of sound, always intentional, elevates the poem's satirical bite without detracting from its deeper commentary. The Effect is a keenly ironic yet mordantly humorous critique of vanity, greed, and the hollow rituals of outmoded traditions. The poem urges the reader to reconsider the significance of symbols and honors, particularly when they become estranged from their original purpose or meaning, a subtlety lingering after the final line.

The Poetess: The two oldest paid professions for women are maid and prostitute. Women tend to hire maids to help with housework, and men tend to hire prostitutes for sexual gratification The theft switch of expensive real jewelry with fake folderol jewelry reveals the envy of a maid, masked in fake servility to a queen. Here, it is an act of revenge against a queen by a trusted maid, seen as full of stupidity, but who is also the one greedy with cupidity. The ancient foreign French phrase 'fol-de-roi' means 'folly of a king' or nonsense, cheap costume ornamentation. The garter on a woman's thigh is an intimate sexual item; yet here, if a knight puts it on a queen -- an act of romantic chivalry. To gentlemen, women can be sexual and romantic as ladies. Men marry women who can perform both functions, domesticated as wives and maids.

Poem 148: DWA

Domestic Workers Association
(Secretly duty with authority)
Supports domestic rights. Legal faction
Formed by generous lawyers, they take pity
On nannies without money. Such cases
Involving: abuse, overtime, no pay,
Illegal entry, no work papers, less
Pay than the minimum wage, no free day,
Are reviewed case by case by staff lawyer,
Legal support and volunteer workers,
Who advise the domestics together
In their best interests. Each nanny swears
She can deserve and know her legal rights.
They volunteer. DWA fights!

Analysis Poem 148: DWA

The Structure of the poem is a series of tightly constructed quatrains, each offering a snapshot of the legal advocacy work provided by the Domestic Workers Association. The poem's ordered form contrasts with the chaotic and often exploitative circumstances it describes, with its rhythmic precision subtly reflecting the legal process — methodical, repetitive, and, at times, grinding.

The Meaning centers on the poignant exploration of the often invisible labor of domestic workers and the systemic injustices they endure. Through careful enumeration of the grievances — abuse, unpaid overtime, lack of legal documentation, and substandard wages — the poetess underscores the relentless vulnerability of these workers, who are persistently denied their rights. The Domestic Workers Association's role, though vital, is framed not as a grand, altruistic gesture, but as a necessary yet Sisyphean effort against a system that perpetuates inequity.

The Imagery in the poem is stark and unembellished, presenting domestic labor as a realm fraught with precariousness and exploitation. Phrases such as 'Illegal entry' and 'no work papers' paint a bleak portrait of workers suspended in a precarious existence, stripped of legal protections and rendered susceptible to systemic mistreatment. Rather than romanticizing their plight, the poem employs a raw, almost clinical depiction, compelling readers to confront unsettling realities of invisible struggles.

Literary devices in the poem intricately reveal the layers of systemic injustice. Power phrases, such as 'Legal faction' and the workers' conditions, create a rhythmic emphasis that underscores key themes and draws attention to the institutional mechanisms at play. The effect of the poem is both intellectual and visceral. It demands an examination of the inequities within our societal structures, compelling the reader to question the very systems that purport to protect but ultimately neglect the most vulnerable.

The Poetess: Rich lawyers helping poor victims win is a conscionable act toward class inequality. Victims of class bias are often the poor, taken advantage of by rich employers who underpay and overwork. But the poor could possibly steal when living in, as domestics. Homecare programs attract many foreign women to work and immigrate to care for seniors, disabled, sick, and children. I wonder if my friend Attorney Alias would help fight for the rights of maids, nannies, caregivers, and all domestic workers -- pro bono publico -- for the sake of justice? (Pronounce generous as gen'-rous.)
I work as a Home Care Aide with agencies. At DWA, I used my Legal Secretary training as a volunteer Intake Agent.

Poem 149: Social Medical Housework

Society's ills, analyzed case stu*dies*

Are done by social workers for cl*ients*

Learned in colleges, universi*ties*.

Nurses and caregivers helping pat*ients*

In foster care homes, write their short rep*orts*

For each sick client-patient in a l*og*

Book: noting down incidents, rude ret*orts*,

Activities, routines, a missing c*og*

In mental processes. Any vict*im*

Undergoes physical, mental reh*ab*

With these wonder workers, who with great v*im*

And vigor, lighten up residents' dr*ab*

Lives. Please take courses in soci*ology*,

Medicine, housekeeping, and psych*ology*.

Analysis: Poem 149: Social-Medical Housework

The Structure of the poem is methodical, with stanzas arranged in a balanced rhythm that lends a sense of steadiness to the reading experience. The use of enjambment allows ideas to flow naturally across lines, creating a seamless progression that avoids rigidity. The poem's pacing alternates between deliberate pauses and fluid transitions, which also mirrors the ebb and flow of the caregivers' work.

The Meaning of the poem delves into the complexities of caregiving, shedding light on the paradox of emotional investment within a bureaucratic framework. Through references to the act of 'noting down incidents' and documenting 'a missing cog / In mental processes', the poetess exposes the tension between the caregivers' compassionate engagement and the cold, mechanistic nature of their work. The Imagery masterfully oscillates between the detached and the intimate, illustrating the dichotomy of caregiving. Terms such as 'write their short reports' and 'in a log / Book' evoke a mechanized, bureaucratic approach, while 'lighten up residents' drab / Lives' introduces a more tender, human element. The poetess has also experienced being a caregiver for seniors and children.

The poem employs a range of Literary devices that enhance its thematic depth. Metaphor and alliteration are used subtly, as the caregivers are referred to as 'wonder workers', likening their demanding labor to something almost magical, yet underscoring how little actual wonder is involved in the process. The synecdoche in referring to the caregivers' actions as mere 'reports' and 'log / Book' distills their labor into cold documentation, stripping away the rich, human experience behind it. Through these devices, the poem unveils the dissonance between the caregivers' vital emotional contributions and society's reduction of them to mechanical roles, inviting the reader to reflect on the true value of their work. The Effect of the poem is both thought-provoking and evocative. Her restraint in language reflects her mastery — she trusts the reader to understand the significance of each word, relying on implication rather than direct exposition.

The Poetess: Social work and medical healthcare are funded and subsidized by public taxes, lotteries, and discounted premium fees in North America. Women dominate both social work and healthcare; men dominate the police, fire, navy, army, and air force services. These public services are meant to help the public when needed for retirement, unemployment, sickness, disability, protection, and emergencies. American taxpayers know that these are allocated as paycheck deductions for Social Services and Medicare, along with federal, state, and municipal taxes. Often, recipients and patients are served by social workers, nurses, and caregivers. A willingness to help, the sick, elderly, disabled, and poor, suggests an apt personality for these healthcare professions. (Pronounce sociology as so-cio-lo-gy.)

CHAPTER 2
Wealth and Poverty Explanation

Society's class systems exist to structure and organize civilizations, particularly in this material world — often constrained by money and physical limitations. In this third book, the poetess explores, through both imagination and experience, how class mentality shapes the personalities and relationships of the characters in her sonnet stories. Having lived both extremes, she brings a unique perspective — experiencing wealth in childhood due to her parents' upbringing and later facing poverty through her own efforts as an adult. Whether her portrayals of these class-based personalities are truthful and believable is open to interpretation, as social status can shift with income, education, marriage, or sheer imagination.

In certain societies, such as England and India, class and caste systems dictate one's place from birth, often without the possibility of change. Education, employment, business, marriage, or even crime cannot always alter social standing. An individual is born into a position, lives within it, and ultimately dies in it — whether this is predetermined before birth remains a matter of speculation, often explained by karma and the morality of cause and effect. Yet, in some parts of the world, class mobility is possible. Love, for instance, can bridge even the widest divides, while luck can sometimes alter one's fortune and lifestyle. Many national lotteries thrive on the dreams of those who believe in a sudden twist of fate, though winning is rare.

Fiction and fantasy fuel romantic ideals, like the timeless Cinderella tale, where a girl rises from rags to riches when a prince falls in love with her. In reality, however, social mobility varies — some countries provide opportunities to climb the economic ladder through education and employment, while others do not. Readers judge for themselves, reflecting on how class and caste have shaped their own identities and perceptions.

This brings us to the poetess' online romance with her fantasy, PJ MacAmour, who in reality is vastly different from her in wealth and success — a classic case of opposites attracting, fascinated by their differences. Their relationship exists purely in the realm of creative imagination, nurtured by social media chatting, messaging, and the exchange of photos and video selfies. One can only wonder what will happen when they finally meet and confront the stark reality of lived experience. Certainly, Amelia Alias, her girlfriend, will help judge his suitability as a boyfriend, although he could expect to be pursued instead, as most famous singer-musician rockstars by their fanatics... I wonder whether she prefers being chased, too?

As a disembodied, non-physical, and spiritual entity — her guide and analyst — I, Professor Gerrymander, have observed her struggles in the material plane without ever experiencing them myself. This detachment allows me to analyze her with clarity, unaffected by the constraints of physical existence. This poetry book presents characters shaped by their economic backgrounds, their thoughts and actions influenced by the realities of their class. Yet, as history has shown, appearances can be deceiving — a millionaire may be a miser, while a pauper may pose as a prince. Creatives and intellectuals, in particular, sometimes escape material limitations, protected in societies like America, where their contributions to culture and knowledge are valued as intellectual properties with residual royalties.

Wealth and Poverty was the third modern sonnet book about how money and power can change character and lifestyle. Money can be earned, won, inherited, married into, shared and stolen.

Poem 1: Wealth and Poverty

1.	*Des-ti-ny from birth may be blessed or <u>cursed</u>*	*A*
2.	*By one's past life-times, per-so-na-<u>li-ty</u>,*	*B*
3.	*And back-ground. Old life scripts might be re-h<u>earsed</u>*	*A*
4.	*Un-til re-solved or es-ta-blished. Pi-<u>ty</u>*	*B*
5.	*If one's path leads to no-where. To be b<u>orn</u>*	*C*
6.	*Rich or poor may be but the be-<u>gin-ning</u>,*	*D*
7.	*Not the end. Whe-ther one has pride or sc<u>orn</u>*	*C*
8.	*For one's ac-com-plish-ments, lo-sing, w<u>in-ning</u>,*	*D*
9.	*Is due to will, skill and luck. Some walk r<u>oads</u>*	*E*
10.	*Full of rocks and stones that block one's pro-<u>gress</u>;*	*F*
11.	*O-thers walk on pave-ments. What-e-ver g<u>oads</u>*	*E*
12.	*One to make this turn or take that e-<u>gress</u>*	*F*
13.	*Is puz-zling. To es-cape dire po-v<u>ert-y</u>,*	*G*
14.	*En-joy wealth, work, and main-tain pro-p<u>er-ty</u>.*	*G*

Analysis Poem 1: Wealth and Poverty

The Structure of the poem is intricately designed to mirror the flux of destiny itself. The steady cadence of quatrains, flowing yet deliberate, serves as a subtle backdrop to the chaotic force of fate that the poem contemplates. The transitions between thoughts feel almost seamless, as if the poetess were reflecting on each idea in real time, with no hurry to reach a conclusion. In its Meaning, the poem opens an expansive meditation on the unpredictability of life, framing destiny as a complex dance between inherent traits (past lives, personality) and external circumstances (wealth, poverty).

In terms of Imagery, the poem introduces two striking visual contrasts. The 'roads / Full of rocks and stones' conjures a vision of hardship, suggesting the burdens that obstruct progress, while the 'pavements' evoke ease and privilege, symbolizing the smoother paths afforded to some. This vivid imagery allows the reader to viscerally experience the disparity between struggle and privilege. The simplicity of these images belies their depth, offering a clear yet powerful commentary on social inequality.

The Literary devices employed throughout the poem further enrich its thematic exploration. For instance, through alliteration in 'wealth, work' and rhyme in 'losing, winning', the poem introduces a melodic quality that draws attention to the fluctuations of fortune, underscoring the unpredictable nature of life's outcomes. There is also a subtle irony in the poem's reflection on destiny. While the poem describes how certain factors may influence one's path, it simultaneously highlights the inherent randomness of life. The Effect on the reader is one of introspection and contemplation. The poem forces the reader to consider their role in shaping their destiny, while also acknowledging the external forces that influence one's journey. This skillful orchestration of thought and form showcases the author's refined craft and intellectual acuity.

The Poetess: The economic class one is born into is one's stepping stone in life, built on one's parents' achievements. Some are blessed with being born rich and continue on in the same class. Some are cursed and suffer the twists of the wheel of fortune, losing their wealth somehow, from wars, bankruptcy, disinheritance, to fraud and crime. Others manage to reverse their poor class status through hard work, education, intelligence, opportunity, fortune, and marriage. Many more achieve the middle class, usually through marriage and employment. Personality and lifestyle are closely associated in a cause and effect relationship with money. It also affects relationships. 'Money makes the world go round', as the song goes, or as the wedding vow, 'for richer, for poorer', it can test love's endurance and flexibility.
Born upper middle class, but my professional self and lifestyle are working class, changing with each job and apartment. I am also in business class because of IO Media, a video television movie production and advertising channel.

Poem 2: Ersatz Escort

For Eme, dating girls was an escapade.
A rich bachelor turned escape artist.
He wriggled out of dates through a decade
By traveling to cities: Rome, Tunis,
Paris, New York, Jakarta, Manila
And Toledo. He refused to escort
Heiresses dressed in ersatz chinchilla
On a ski lodge, nor at a beach resort
Like Boracay with actresses in thongs,
Showing off more skin than clothing. Marriage
Was a state he abhorred, as crowds or throngs.
To him, "Two is a crowd. Trapped in a cage
With a female tiger, I would throttle
Her more likely than live in married hell!"

Analysis Poem 2: Ersatz Escort

The Structure of the poem mirrors its central theme of evasion, employing a steady yet dynamic rhythm to reflect Erne's constant movement away from commitment. The alternating rhyme scheme adds a sense of balance and control to the narrative, contrasting sharply with the chaos of his romantic escapades. This structural precision enhances the poem's wit, underscoring the absurdity of Erne's choices while maintaining a refined poetic balance.

The Meaning delves into Erne's disdain for societal conventions, particularly those surrounding love and marriage. Through his escapades across cities and continents, the poem portrays Erne as a modern-day libertine, valuing freedom above all. His avoidance of relationships, symbolized by his rejection of 'Heiresses' and 'actresses', reveals his deep aversion to perceived constraints of intimacy and marital life.

The Imagery in the poem is vivid and evocative, painting a picture of glamorous settings and extravagant characters. Cities like 'Rome, Tunis, / Paris, New York' evoke a sense of adventure and freedom, while specific details — such as 'ersatz chinchilla' and 'actresses in thongs' — create striking visual contrasts between high society's ostentatious display and Erne's indifference to it.

The Literary devices enrich the poem's playful yet incisive tone. Hyperbole is skillfully employed in 'Trapped in a cage / With a female tiger' exaggerating Erne's dread of marriage to almost comical levels, yet underscoring the intensity of his feelings. While the irony embedded in his lavish, escapist lifestyle highlights the absurdity of his refusal to embrace deeper connections, even as he pursues fleeting pleasures. The Effect on the reader is one of amusement mixed with contemplation. The expert blending of satire and insight ensures that the poem entertains while subtly encouraging the reader to reflect on their own values and the societal norms that shape them.

The Poetess: Wealthy families are often concerned about marrying into the same class, so they often arrange marriages for their heirs to ensure their family wealth continues growing like a business expansion. Some heirs do try dating anyone they are interested in; however, if it becomes serious, their parents will intervene, advise against it, and even block the marriage. Some are satisfied with remaining single and avoid dating, mating, and marriage. They feel no obligation to find a spouse and continue their family name with children. Self-love and independence are more important. The modern goal for a marriage is to have a dual income household, both individuals work, independent from parents' wealth and control. Celibate singlehood is my main mode in personal life -- although I dated, mated, and lived with others, I never married...

Poem 5: False-Hearted Juju

Juju over-indulged in food, 'Methinks
I need a wife, perhaps demi-mondaine
Who can support my gluttony with chinks.
Thus, I'd be above such matters mundane
As rent, food, utility bills.' In Church,
He prayed for such a wife and finally
His prayers were answered. 'I need not search
Further. Elda seems gullible. Dally
No more and propose.' Within 3 quick months,
They moved in together, sharing the bills.
She soon supported him, despite her taunts
At his ineptness. Her nagging sent chills
Through him, 'She's like every woman, hateful
When the tables are turned, with a mouthful!'

Analysis Poem 5: False-Hearted Juju

The Structure of the poem is methodical, reflecting Juju's calculated and pragmatic worldview. The consistent rhyme scheme mirrors his step-by-step strategy to secure a partner, while the smooth progression of lines contrasts with the discord that eventually arises in his relationship.

The Meaning unravels the selfish motivations underpinning Juju's desire for a partner, turning the notion of marriage into a critique of convenience and exploitation. By portraying love as a means to an end — a tool for escaping responsibilities like bills and rent — the poem exposes the hollowness of such relationships. Juju's disillusionment when faced with Elda's reproaches further illustrates the consequences of reducing human connections to transactions.

The Imagery in the poem is sharp and evocative, bringing to life Juju's gluttony and eventual frustration. Lines such as 'support my gluttony with chinks' vividly depict his unapologetic self-indulgence, while 'nagging sent chills' captures the tension and emotional toll of their union. The employment of stark and unembellished visual language ensures that the imagery cuts through with clarity and impact reinforcing the satire.

The Literary devices add depth to the poem's humor and critique. Irony is woven throughout, from Juju's prayer for a partner in a sacred space to his later resentment of the very relationship he sought. This irony underscores the futility and selfishness of his goals. Hyperbole is evident in lines like 'sent chills / Through him', exaggerating his discomfort to both humorous and critical effect. The Effect on the reader is one of both amusement and subtle unease. Juju's brazen selfishness and eventual downfall elicit laughter, while the underlying critique of exploitative dynamics fosters reflection. The poetess' evolution is evident in her ability to seamlessly intertwine sharp satire with layered introspection.

The Poetess: Men are stereotypically the breadwinners, earning more than women even in this modern age. However, there are men who are unable to be in this higher-income position, so they search for women who earn more and date them. Women tend not to initiate mating nor marrying, and wait for men for either a proposition or a proposal. Love and compatibility can also influence decisions, along with practical financial reasons. When the female partner earns more than the male partner, this role reversal of stereotypical gender expectations can be a cause of domestic arguments. This is unfair nowadays, to continue expecting men to support women more because both can be working and sharing expenses in living -- meals, utility bills, accommodation, transportation, etc.

Poem 8: Slumbering Slums

Big cities everywhere have their poor slums
Which barely shelter people within walls
Of wood and stone. Unemployed, homeless bums
Wander streets, lost, longing for things in malls
And department stores. Maybe they do sleep
The slumber of helpless, impoverished
Ignorance, or an innocence to weep
By? Education, employment, cherished
By the middle class are non-existent
For some, a lack of opportunity --
The root of why they live impermanent
Nomadic lives. Subsistence in city
Slums is a pathetic result from lack
Of urban planning or plain old bad luck!

Analysis Poem 8: Slumbering Slums

The Structure of the poem adheres to a tightly controlled rhythm and rhyme scheme that effectively conveys a sense of inevitability and despair. The alternating rhymes, though simple, create a steady cadence that mirrors the monotonous and cyclical nature of poverty. The Meaning of the poem reveals a pointed critique of urban neglect and inequitable systems that perpetuate poverty. It paints a picture of a world in which the disadvantaged are relegated to the periphery, existing in a state of precariousness and deprivation. The poem emphasizes the disconnect between the impoverished and the affluent, specifically highlighting the absence of education and employment opportunities, which are the pillars of social mobility for the middle class.

The Imagery throughout the poem is sharp, evocative, and haunting in its simplicity. The image of 'walls / Of wood and stone' presents a raw, physical reality of makeshift homes — fragile and vulnerable, yet firmly entrenched in their poverty. The 'slumber of helpless, impoverished / Ignorance' serves as both a literal and metaphorical representation of the marginalized, suggesting that the absence of opportunity results in a kind of passive surrender. The imagery here is striking in its rawness — there is nothing sentimental about the way of describing poverty and deprivation. Yet, that is exactly what makes it so compelling and thought-provoking.

The Literary devices employed in the poem include irony and personification. The ironic juxtaposition of the homeless 'longing for things in malls' next to their harsh reality serves to emphasize the disparity between society's surface-level pleasures and the deep-rooted issues faced by those in poverty. Personification is present in the root of poverty, which is identified as a lack of opportunity — an abstract concept that takes on an almost monstrous form, becoming the cause of all their suffering. The Effect on the reader is one of discomfort mixed with deep reflection. The poem does not seek to evoke pity for its subjects but rather urges the reader to question the forces that perpetuate such inequality.

The Poetess: Urban development in big cities offers many jobs and rental apartments to immigrants and citizens. Working-class singles often find this setup of living and working in the same city. Middle-class couples with children buy houses in nearby suburban development areas. But even in wealthy nations, there are people who are unemployed, uneducated, unskilled, and may have health problems, such as mental and physical disabilities, alcohol and drug addiction, or a past criminal conviction -- resulting in homelessness and poverty. Poor nations have even more socio-economic factors causing a larger percentage of poor people. Lack of: development, employment, funding, public services, education, skills, and opportunities, with overpopulation, results in urban slums.

Poem 34: House Hunting

Realtors show off houses up for sale
In the neighborhood suburbs. The buyers
Wandering around the houses rate by scale
Of 1 to 10 each house, noting features
That appeal or not. They come in all shapes
And sizes; some are too tall for doorways!
To match a house with owner, from the drapes,
To the carpets is quite a feat. It pays
To know what the buyer wants in a house
Or to expose them to something different
They may not have imagined. Those with spouse
In hand are harder to please; two heads bent
Together may oppose. While house hunting,
Sellers must convince them -- it beats renting!

Analysis Poem 34: House Hunting

The Structure of the poem is meticulously crafted, with a regular rhyme scheme that mimics the transactional nature of the house-buying process. The rhythmic consistency evokes the methodical and sometimes impersonal experience of real estate, where potential buyers evaluate each property with an almost clinical detachment. The poem's use of iambic tetrameter ensures that each stanza flows smoothly, reflecting the routine and predictable movement of the buyers through the house.

The Meaning of the poem extends beyond the simple act of purchasing a home to comment on the deeper motivations and nuances that underlie consumer behavior. The description of buyers as coming in 'all shapes / And sizes, some are too tall for doorways', speaks to the dissonance between the idea of a home as a perfect match for its inhabitants and the often arbitrary process of choosing one. The way she intertwines the transactional elements of real estate with a deeper commentary on human desires shows the sophistication of her evolving poetic voice.

The Imagery in the poem, though grounded in the ordinary act of buying a house, evokes a sense of alienation and distance. The buyers, as described, are 'Wandering around' as if detached from the houses they are considering — almost as if they are tourists in a foreign land, looking for something that might 'appeal or not'. The Literary devices employed in the poem further enrich its layers of meaning. The irony of the house-buying process is encapsulated in the phrase 'rat(ing) by scale / Of 1 to 10', which transforms something as personal as finding a home into a numerical evaluation.

The Effect on the reader is a growing sense of unease, as the poem subtly exposes the hollow nature of consumerist behavior and the dissonance between one's desires and the reality of materialism. This has moved beyond simply documenting the process to critiquing it, peeling back layers to expose the emotional and social dimensions of consumerism.

The Poetess: An exciting stage in middle-class and married life is shopping around for a house! Realtors can show potential buyers the available houses with a scheduled appointment or an open house, where people can just drop by from a front yard sign. A few agents pre-screen based on income to limit curiosity seekers, since they do have to drive over and open the house for viewing. But many popular websites exist online for sellers and buyers -- Zillow, Realtor, Redfin, Trulia, Homes. Viewing is easy, convenient, and free! (Pronounce different as diff'-rent.)

Poem 47: Affluence Flatulence

Eating 'merienda', Flauta felt bloated
By gas, yet continues her light repast
Conversing all the while. Unabated,
Her stomach grumbles. 'I must have bad gas
Trapped in my poor bowels and small innards.
Should I thus excuse myself to my guests
And relieve the gas, or eat more gizzards
And caviar?' She thought. 'These queer requests
For delicacies must be the main cause
Of my gas condition. Should I avoid
Partaking them despite courtesy laws?'
Guests, none the wiser of her paranoid
Speculation, enjoyed her affluence
And generosity with flatulence.

Analysis Poem 47: Affluence Flatulence

The Structure of the poem follows a cyclical rhythm that mirrors Flauta's internal conflict. The steady flow of the verse contrasts sharply with the disruption of her physical discomfort, and the poem's tight rhyme scheme reflects the predictable routine of her social obligations, even while she is increasingly preoccupied by her bodily distress.

The Meaning of the poem delves into the human experience of maintaining societal norms even when they conflict with basic biological needs. Flauta is caught between the pressure to conform to the polite expectations of her guests and the natural instincts of the body. Her choice to present this conflict through humor shows a sophisticated understanding of how human dignity can be strained by the constant pressure to adhere to societal norms.

The Imagery in the poem is both pungent and refined, effectively combining the lavish setting with the discomfort of Flauta's internal world. The contrast between the 'delicacies' and her 'grumbles' illustrates the surreal disconnect between appearance and experience, amplifying the humor while adding layers to the narrative. The Literary devices employed in the poem add texture and depth to Flauta's internal monologue. The repetition of her internal questions — 'Should I thus excuse myself '— creates a rhythm that mirrors her indecision and constant analysis.

The Effect on the reader is one of both amusement and reflection. On one level, the poem provides a humorous account of an uncomfortable social experience, where bodily functions disrupt the smooth flow of high-society norms. On another level, it invites the reader to consider the pressures of conformity in a world that often values appearances over personal authenticity. This evolving sophistication in the poetess' work demonstrates a real maturity in both thematic exploration and technical execution.

The Poetess: When hosting parties, planning the food and drink menu can be a challenge because of the budget, diverse tastes, and dietary restrictions of guests. Serving unusual appetizers with strange ingredients can be a big experimental risk of failing to please guests' palates and appetites. Not every guest will taste dishes with liver, kidney, or intestines -- especially at a party! This poem pokes fun at a hostess who ends up in the embarrassing condition of gas triggered by eating the organs of animals. However, even her polite guests are suffering from the same condition and situation. Between family and close friends, such a personal condition can be a private yet common topic. The ladies' room maintains confidentiality between women. For parties, it would be better to stick to popular, mainstream, and well-known ingredients and items to lessen such a discomforting, distressing dilemma.

Poem 48: Family Parasite

Mel, the black sheep of the family, rogue
And ruffian, was often unemployed
Because he thought, 'It is never in vogue
For a cad to work for someone.' He toyed
With the idea of a small business,
But he decided that using people
Was easier for him, since it was less
Risky. Weaned from his kind mother's nipple,
He progressed to suck as family leach
On his brothers and sisters. Creative,
He painted them in exchange. 'I beseech
Them for room and board. Every relative
Has an ego to be fed. Both recluse
And socialite have no cause to refuse!'

Analysis Poem 48: Family Parasite

The Structure of the poem mirrors Mel's manipulative nature — tight and deliberate, yet with a flowing cadence that makes his scheming feel effortless. The iambic meter reinforces the balance between Mel's deception and the family's reluctant acceptance, creating a steady, almost inevitable march of dependency. The Meaning extends beyond Mel's freeloading to a broader commentary on entitlement and exploitation. He sees himself not as a burden but as someone playing a role, feeding into the egos of those around him in exchange for their support. The phrase 'Every relative / Has an ego to be fed' exposes his sharp awareness of human vanity, suggesting that his manipulation is not merely out of laziness but a calculated strategy.

The Imagery enhances the tension between dependency and resourcefulness. Mel is first described as 'Weaned from his kind mother's nipple', but rather than becoming independent, he simply shifts his parasitic tendencies onto his siblings. This transformation is visual and visceral, portraying his survival as something instinctual, almost primal. There is biting humor here, as the poem refuses to make him a tragic figure; instead, he is almost admirable in his audacity. Yet families do tend to inter-dependency.

The Literary devices strengthen the poem's ironic tone. The juxtaposition of 'Both recluse / And socialite' shows Mel's adaptability — his ability to fit into any situation as long as it benefits him. The self-aware dialogue, such as 'I beseech / Them for room and board', turns his exploitation into something oddly formal, as if his dependency is a form of art rather than a moral failing. The wordplay between 'paint(ing) them' and feeding their egos adds another layer — his contribution to the family is not material but performative. The Effect on the reader is an uneasy amusement. Mel's actions are parasitic, yet his self-awareness and wit make him oddly compelling. The mastery of satire -- humor is not just in the subject, but in the structure, the irony, and the sharp observational wit.

The Poetess: Some families have an oddball family member who does not fit in with the group's values and personalities. This can lead to ostracism, even from their own family, and also out in society. A group, like a family, often has similarities that outnumber their differences, and sharing is often part of the bonding in close relationships. The parasite in this poem is a survivor who, knowing the obligation that families have to take care of their own flesh and blood, uses this duty to manipulate them into supporting him financially in exchange for flattering their egos by painting their portraits. Fortunately, he probably has enough talent for painting people to offer this symbiotic exchange. Or maybe it might be mutualism (both benefit) or commensalism (one benefits, other neutral), rather than parasitism (one benefits, other harmed)?

Poem 53: Unforeseen Clause

Yaz, an actress, worked beyond endurance,
Practising scenes, which she was ill-suited
For. Upon buying some life insurance
One day, she then decided to play dead
And collect the money, as the heiress.
With cohorts who promised to disinter
Her after the quick funeral (unless
She could claw her way out), she thus sent her
Insurance agent notice of her death,
Listing auto accident as the cause.
He attended the burial to bequeath
The money. Tragedy was that a clause
Said the heiress had to be in the hearse
At the same time, which they did not rehearse!

Analysis Poem 53: Unforeseen Clause

The Structure of the poem employs a steady rhyme scheme and controlled meter, which reflects the precision required in both acting and deception, as if the entire poem is a performance itself. Each line builds toward the inevitable irony of the final couplet, where Yaz's lack of rehearsal proves fatal. The Meaning delves into ambition, deception, and the consequences of overconfidence. Yaz is portrayed as someone who pushes herself beyond reason in pursuit of success, yet ironically, chooses fraud as her final act when she realizes her limitations. Rather than making Yaz simply a fool, the poem paints her as a tragicomic figure — bold, determined, but ultimately undone by her own artistry.

The Imagery blends theatrical and morbid elements, making Yaz's fraud feel like an ill-fated stage production. The contrast between 'playing dead' and actually dying is both humorous and unsettling. The mention of her being 'disinter(red)' suggests a macabre resurrection scene, which, when paired with the final irony, turns the poem into a dark farce. The insurance agent, unwittingly attending what he believes is just another business transaction, adds an almost absurd realism to the scene.

The Literary devices amplify the poem's wit. The reference to an 'auto accident' as her cause of death contrasts with the meticulously planned fraud, emphasizing the disconnect between the script she has written for herself and the reality she could not control. The final line is the perfect comedic punch: the clause in the insurance policy turns the entire scheme into a tragic miscalculation. The Effect on the reader is a mix of amusement and grim realization. Yaz's fate is undeniably funny, yet there is an underlying commentary on the lengths people will go to escape failure. Her story is not just about fraud — it is about the illusion of control and the danger of believing one can outmaneuver fate. The poetess has evolved beyond simple storytelling; now, the humor is layered with deeper themes, and the irony is razor-sharp. This is satire at its finest — both entertaining and thought-provoking.

The Poetess: Insurance is common for those who need financial protection against future disasters, damages, diseases, and death. Thus, many agencies sell insurance for: life, healthcare, property, vehicle, professional, and business liabilities. Fraud for financial gain in a faked death and collection of one's own life insurance is a hard feat to pull off. Whether anyone has succeeded is unknown; certainly, unpublished because of copycat crimes. Life insurance until age 65 is useful for those with a spouse and children, although many seniors are outliving their term policies since, nowadays, people live until their 80s, thanks to improvements in healthcare. To act as the dead policyholder and living beneficiary is preposterous and certainly fraudulent.

Poem 48: Business Empires

Industrialization for commercial
Products has enabled mass production
To feed world markets. International
Trade for these goods is an introduction
To business cooperation, world peace,
The global village marketing concept.
Countries that progressed, where vicious wars ceased,
Are busy manufacturing, except
Nuclear or firearms. Some European
Kingdoms established schools and factories
In the world: Asias, Americas and
Soviet states. All developing countries
Profited from this imperialism;
We're by-products of colonialism!

Analysis Poem 48: Business Empires

The Structure of the poem mirrors the efficiency and orderliness of industrial production itself — precise, rhythmic, and unyielding. The controlled meter replicates the mechanical cadence of mass production, while the rhyme scheme imposes a sense of inevitability, much like the global economic systems it describes.

The Meaning delves into the intersection of economic expansion, globalization, and historical legacy. The assertion that 'we're by-products of colonialism' reframes modern development as an extension of past power structures rather than an independent achievement. There is an implicit question here: can global progress ever be fully separated from its imperial roots? Rather than a straightforward endorsement or condemnation, the poem presents a nuanced perspective — progress is real, but so are its historical debts. The Imagery contrasts the symbols of progress with the remnants of conquest, painting a world where factories and schools emerge from the remnants of former empires. The juxtaposition of 'Nuclear or fire arms' with institutions of learning and industry highlights a transformation — once-dominant nations now wield economic and educational influence rather than military force.

The Literary devices reinforce the poem's central themes through subtle wordplay and irony. The phrase 'global village marketing concept' merges ideals of unity with the realities of consumerism, framing diplomacy as an economic strategy rather than a purely moral pursuit. The term 'by-products' in the final line is particularly sharp — it reduces entire nations and peoples to unintended consequences of colonial expansion, mirroring the mechanized nature of industry itself. The Effect on the reader is one of contemplation and subtle unease. Rather than offering a definitive stance, it leaves the reader questioning whether modern prosperity is a genuine evolution or simply a refined version of historical dominance. The poetess' evolving craft is evident in the layered complexity.

The Poetess: Industrial countries such as the Group of 7/8 also known as G7/G8: United States of America, Canada, France, Germany, Italy, Japan, the United Kingdom, and formerly Russia have invented and pioneered technology, mass production, vehicles, and appliances. They also have histories of global imperialism, colonizing less developed countries. The modern world and machines are driving progress in the production of goods, the architecture of properties, and the engineering of vehicles. Thanks to trade, less developed countries are able to buy machinery, equipment, and technology products to achieve a modern lifestyle; developed industrialized countries, also have factories in these countries with cheaper labor, opening markets globally. (Pronounce industrialization as in-dus-tr'a-li-za-tion.)
With IO Media channel, I attended as a Videographer at the G20 Summit hosted in Toronto, Ontario, Canada, in 2010.

Poem 81: Python in Phaeton

Steyn expects obedience as instructor
Of his wife, Deirdra. Born to a wealthy
Family, he purchased a constrictor,
A python to strangle her if fealty
Is not observed by her. Under the seat
Of the phaeton, he keeps it. "Our marriage
Is satisfactory, I hope?" The heat
Inside stirs the serpent in the carriage.
"Of course, Mister Stone. I am quite content
With the house, our lifestyle, our sacred vows.
You rescued me from struggles, discontent,
And I am grateful." "Do you think that cows
Go mad when their bulls wander far away,
With mouths frothing, getting sores, while at play?"

Analysis Poem 81: Python in Phaeton

The Structure of the poem is tightly wound. Each line builds a quiet but escalating tension, with the final couplet delivering a sinister shift from veiled threat to outright psychological manipulation. The structure reinforces the sense of entrapment — Deirdra's life is measured, controlled, and, much like the poem itself, inescapably dictated by Steyrn's will.

The Meaning unearths themes of control, fear, and the illusion of marital harmony. Steyrn's power is not just financial but psychological, his wealth granting him authority over Deirdra in a way that is both tangible and symbolic. The presence of the python is more than just a physical threat — it represents the silent, constant pressure that ensures her obedience. Her compliance is framed as gratitude, yet the entire exchange reeks of coercion. The Imagery is rich with oppression and dread, blending elements of wealth and menace into a single, suffocating tableau. The juxtaposition of lavish comfort 'house, lifestyle, sacred vows' with the lurking, coiled menace undercuts the illusion of stability, emphasizing that Deirdra's security is entirely conditional. The contrast between civility and coercion heightens the poem's unease — there is no dramatic outburst, only an unbearable quiet in which compliance is the only option.

The Literary devices reinforce the unsettling nature of the poem. The irony in "rescued me from struggles" is biting, as her escape from hardship has only placed her in a more refined form of subjugation. The final rhetorical question is the most sinister device of all, transforming a deeply personal fear into a detached metaphor about livestock, effectively stripping Deirdra of individuality. The Effect on the reader is one of growing discomfort. The absence of overt conflict makes the underlying horror more insidious, as control here is not enforced through physical force but through unrelenting, inescapable pressure. The mastery of subtext is evident; rather than delivering a straightforward critique, the poem thrives in its subtleties.

The Poetess: Coverture was a male-gender-biased system wherein a woman lost some rights to her husband after marriage -- rights to own property, enter contracts, exercise autonomy, and keep custody of children. Women were chattel like cattle. The wealthy class tends to marry within their own, but some might marry outside their level. The expectations of a wealthy man supporting a poorer woman can be her obedience, loyalty, and domesticity. His jealousy and protection could mean a restriction of her freedom. Some wives accept this ownership and treatment, being faithful and obligated for such support, especially if they no longer need to work outside and marry into a higher economic and social class. This poem is written about the era prior to 1839 when the Married Women's Property Act changed laws for married women state by state, and eventually, in America and Great Britain. Attorney Alias probably advocated for equality in her marriage.

Poem 84: Homemaking Hermit

Applying for a work visa to <u>leave</u>
At whatever cost, Ermi switched car<u>eer</u>
To that of homemaker. Cleaning, a <u>peeve</u>
Task she disliked, she learned, and not one <u>tear</u>
Did she drop, for hopes of wealth and free<u>dom</u>
In foreign lands. Landing in Cana<u>da</u>,
She was hired by an employer: hands<u>ome</u>,
Rich, single. He smiled,"Ikaw magan<u>da</u>",
Which he learned in evening Tagalog c<u>lass</u>.
She was surprised but delighted. G<u>rinning</u>,
He carried her bags, "We shall attend m<u>ass</u>
Soon and marry, or there will be <u>sinning</u>
Done." They soon filed for a marriage pe<u>rmit</u>
With her as domesticated he<u>rmit</u>.

Analysis Poem 84: Homemaking Hermit

The Structure of the poem is tight, almost transactional. The pacing is controlled, mimicking both the bureaucracy Ermi navigates and the inevitability of her choices. The final couplet solidifies her transformation from an independent seeker of opportunity to a 'domesticated hermit', a shift that feels both abrupt and foreseen. The Meaning delves into migration, sacrifice, and the often-overlooked nuances of dependency. Ermi's decision to become a homemaker is not driven by passion but by necessity; it is a calculated step toward a greater goal. Yet, once abroad, the dynamic shifts — her employer, who initially represents opportunity, swiftly assumes the role of a suitor, dictating her future under the guise of charm.

The Imagery heightens the contrast between aspiration and reality. The foreign land is not depicted as a place of abundance but rather as a setting where Ermi's personal desires must be molded to fit a new role. The employer's Tagalog phrase, "Ikaw maganda" (you are beautiful), is both endearing and performative, hinting at an attempt to bridge cultural gaps while still maintaining control. The poem's skill in weaving subtle foreshadowing is striking — every action, even the seemingly benign ones, is layered with deeper implications. The Literary devices sharpen the poem's underlying critique. The juxtaposition of 'Cleaning, a peeve / Task' with the grandeur of 'hopes of wealth and freedom' highlights the gap between what she desires and what she endures. The employer's final statement, "or there will be sinning / Done", injects humor while exposing an underlying pressure — his intentions are presented as practical, yet there is an implicit demand that Ermi conform to his expectations.

The Effect on the reader is a mix of intrigue and amusement, with an undercurrent of bittersweet acceptance. Ermi's journey carries a sense of achievement — she set out with a goal and seemingly attained it — but the final lines introduce an ambiguity that lingers. The poetess' evolution shines in this restraint — the satire is softer, more insidious.

The Poetess: Interracial, intercultural, and interreligious marriages exist because of increased tourism and immigration between countries. Certain occupations that became high in demand, such as nursing and caregiving, open immigration via employment to many women who dominate those jobs in healthcare. Some women switch careers just to emigrate from countries like Philippines because Canada and America opened employer-sponsored programs in nursing and caregiving, since people are living longer nowadays. Care, being an aspect of love and marriage, makes it understandable why men could marry women employed as nurses or caregivers, or sponsor foreigners for personal care in their own homes, and then marry them too.
I work as a live-out Home Care Aide / Caregiver in senior clients' homes and retirement facilities, and my sisters were Nurses in hospitals and clinics.

Poem 90: Poignant Philanthropy

Sensitive, Suf practiced philan<u>thropy</u>
To assuage her guilt for being born <u>rich</u>.
"Though the world's decaying by en<u>tropy</u>,
I must do my part to preserve it, wh<u>ich</u>
I do by donating to char<u>ities.</u>
I pity the homeless, helpless, poor, s<u>ick</u>
People." In her spare time, she made cook<u>ies</u>
For teas, gave clothes and money (not plas<u>tic</u>).
She helped a lush kick his habit. Poi<u>gnant</u>
Observation of drug and drink ad<u>dicts</u>
Made this her mission. Booz got her preg<u>nant</u>
When he recovered, and they married w<u>eeks</u>
Later. Motto: 'Prefer lone so<u>litude</u>
Or accept payment from soli<u>citude</u>.'

Analysis Poem 90: Poignant Philanthropy

The Structure of the poem consists of steady quatrains and gives the impression of order and intentionality, much like Suf's approach to philanthropy. However, the final couplet introduces an abrupt shift, suggesting a deeper, more ironic reality beneath her altruism. The Meaning of this poem revolves around the intersection of privilege, guilt, and the transactional nature of charity. Suf's philanthropy is framed as an act of atonement rather than genuine connection — her giving serves to ease her conscience more than to transform the lives of those she helps. Her eventual entanglement with Booz, the addict she rehabilitates, reveals an ironic reversal: rather than saving him, she is absorbed into his chaotic world.

The Imagery provides a contrast between Suf's carefully curated acts of charity — 'cookies / For teas…clothes', and financial aid — and the unpredictable outcome of her persona choices, highlights the unpredictability of human relationships. The phrase 'Booz got her pregnant' is stark and jarring, stripping away the illusion of control and exposing the raw consequences of her interactions. The Literary devices in this poem reinforce its central irony — she sets out to heal others but becomes entangled in the very struggles she seeks to alleviate. The phrase 'Prefer lone solitude / Or accept payment from solicitude' serves as both a personal motto and a bitter reflection on the transactional nature of relationships, suggesting that even generosity has an implicit cost.

The Effect of this poem is to leave the reader questioning whether charity can ever be truly selfless. The use of dry humor and irony transforms what could have been a simple moral lesson into a sharp critique of social responsibility, privilege, and unintended consequences.

The Poetess: There are wealthy women and men who practise philanthropy, donating to charities and non-profit organizations, volunteering for causes, and spreading awareness with their actions. Societal problems and issues such as: poverty, homelessness, hunger, disabilities, diseases, and even alcohol and drug addictions, criminal convictions, are concerns that intrigue their conscience. Being born rich and privileged seems to be a conscionable reason for this polar attraction to those who are poor and problematic -- savior or super heroine mentality driving them to save those suffering in society. This interaction can open opportunities for building relationships, perhaps even friendship or marriage. This sonnet shows how acting like a social worker and do-gooder on a salvation mission can attract the person one has saved. Hypogamy, from the rich person's viewpoint, is marrying someone of a lower class, and hypergamy, from the poor person's viewpoint, is to someone higher class; these are really two sides of the same marriage partnership. Adding to this socioeconomic difference, an addiction problem wherein one partner salvages the other can mean lifelong gratitude and duty to each other. Isogamy of equals is not the only factor in choosing a spouse. Pregnancy can trigger a proposal!

Poem 96: Sycophant Hierophant

Creative from childhood, Syko has dreams
Of castles and queens. As a mock princess,
She practises nods, curtsies, high-pitched screams
Of delight, pouring tea, covering chest
When disturbed, and accepting visitors.
She covers her precious mouth while yawning,
Uses tissues sneezing, does all her chores
Without being told, all by mid-morning.
A bookworm, she reads voluminously
Poetry, psychology, and occult
Books, ditto the Bible religiously.
Worshipping gods, goddesses like a cult
Fanatic labeled her a sycophant;
To kings and queens, she is a hierophant.

Analysis Poem 96: Sycophant Hierophant

The Structure of the poem consists of tight quatrains, which reinforce Syko's disciplined, rehearsed mannerisms. The rhythmic precision mimics her meticulous devotion to etiquette and structured learning, while the final couplet presents a shift — from mere admiration to a deeper, almost priestly reverence. The Meaning of the poem highlights a critique of how unchecked admiration can evolve into obsession, eroding individuality and distorting perception. Syko's devotion to royalty and spiritual texts borders on the fanatical, making her less of an independent thinker and more of a devoted follower. Her transformation from 'mock princess' to a self-styled hierophant suggests complete immersion into the world she admires, with no separation between reality and fantasy.

The Imagery contrasts between Syko's structured, disciplined behavior of 'curtsies, high-pitched screams' and her intellectual pursuits of 'Poetry, psychology, and occult / Books', painting a complex portrait of someone trying to mold herself into an idealized figure. Her use of tissues, careful yawning, and obsessive reading habits create a caricature of rigid self-discipline bordering on delusion. The Literary devices include irony in the phrase 'ditto the Bible religiously', which highlights the extent of her all-encompassing devotion — she does not engage with texts critically but absorbs them wholesale. The shift in the final couplet, where she goes from sycophant to hierophant, employs wordplay to show how admiration can transform into unquestioning devotion, raising questions about authority, identity, and self-worth.

The Effect of the poem is that it leaves the reader feeling amused and unsettled. Syko's obsessive mimicry raises deeper questions about identity formation and the dangers of blind reverence. The poem's controlled humor prevents the piece from becoming overtly critical, instead, allowing readers to draw their own conclusions about the fine line between admiration and fanaticism. Being the Poetess' devoted psychophant, our mental telepathy saves my madness.

The Poetess: The State and the Church are the foundations of hierarchy, power, and wealth. In some countries with royalty, those two are one family, leading two institutions controlling their subjects -- under the belief in the God-given right to rule. In Arthurian legend, King Arthur had a magician, Merlin, as his adviser on personal, private, and professional public matters. Intertwining religion, occult, and magic with royal government decisions and affairs, especially in England, which had Wicca as an ancient pagan religion, is still acceptable, albeit secretively now because of Christianity. The Ouija board spells in American English and has occult, pagan symbols, useful as a tool for communicating with spirits, angels, demons, gods, and goddesses. Some people from childhood are psychic and balance pagan occult with modern religion. Some governments acknowledge occult symbols of power in political influences, like God's all-seeing eye in money.

Poem 125: Oscars' Glamor

The peak of acting in famed Holly<u>wood</u>
Reaches frenzy at the Acade<u>my</u>
Awards. Larger than life, each feeling, m<u>ood</u>
Fleeting on flickering film. "Look at <u>me</u>,
I'm a star!" attitude ingrained in <u>all</u>
The members from actors and actre<u>sses</u>,
Technicians, directors, producers. Sm<u>all</u>
Time or big time, everyone rehear<u>ses</u>
For the spotlight, public and ca<u>mera</u>!
High fashion — outrageous to classic b<u>lack</u>
Covers each form, creating chi<u>mera</u>
And charisma. No brown potato <u>sack</u>
Dress in sight. Growing as a wild ru<u>mor</u>,
Fame spreads with each glittering gown's gla<u>mor</u>!

Analysis Poem 125: Oscars' Glamor

The Structure of the poem consists of measured quatrains, reflecting the polished, rehearsed nature of the Oscars event itself. The rhythm mirrors the steady rise of anticipation, while the final couplet delivers a celebratory flourish, encapsulating the spectacle of fame and fashion. The Meaning explores the ephemeral nature of celebrity, the performance of glamour, and the illusion of prestige at the Academy Awards. The Oscars serve as the pinnacle of Hollywood recognition, yet the poem suggests that beneath the spectacle, the pursuit of fame is rehearsed, fleeting, and ultimately performative. The final couplet emphasizes how fame is both an organic and manufactured force, spreading like wildfire but always dictated by appearances.

The Imagery of the poem is rich in contrasts — from the 'flickering film' to the 'glittering gown', it captures the transient magic of Hollywood. The phrase 'no brown potato sack / Dress in sight' humorously underscores the industry's emphasis on presentation, where even perceived authenticity is curated. The mention of 'chimera / And charisma' cleverly ties together illusion and allure, suggesting that both are necessary components of stardom. The "Look at me, / I'm a star!" mentality is portrayed as universal in Hollywood, subtly critiquing the self-importance and homogeneity of the industry. The Literary devices include juxtaposition, which contrasts 'outrageous' fashion and 'classic black', reflecting how the Oscars thrive on both excess and tradition. Metaphors are also utilized, such as the 'wild rumor' of fame spreading, reinforcing Hollywood's dependence on publicity and spectacle rather than genuine artistic merit.

The Effect leaves the reader with a sense of both admiration and skepticism. While it celebrates the grandeur of the Oscars, it also exposes the performative and image-obsessed nature of Hollywood. The poem's playful tone ensures that the critique remains light, inviting readers to revel in the glamour while questioning its substance.

The Poetess: Los Angeles, California, the city that built a global movie empire called Hollywood, continues to be the pioneer of the cinema industry. Actors and actresses who become stars are celebrated during their annual Oscars award night. Television broadcasts the glamorous gowns and tuxedos of the beautiful and handsome movie stars whose faces have become famous, bringing fortune to established studios. The front end cast and the back end crew celebrate this night, hoping their production will win some of the best awards: picture, actor, actress, director, writer, cinematography, music soundtrack, visual effects, etcetera. It does take teamwork and collaboration for every production to succeed. Hollywood and its Oscar awards reward the movies that deserve public attention. Attorney Alias worked in L.A. County.
In the Eighties, I worked as a background movie Extra in Hollywood movies filmed in Vancouver B.C. -- Hollywood North.

Poem 127: Bankrupt Bureaucracy

Taxes collected were appropriated
To the various ministries and projects.
Any surplus went to pay elated
Government employees and the rejects
On welfare. The development programs
For transportation, housing, medical,
Employment, education caused tantrums
In business circles wanting practical
Use of their taxes. Entrepreneurship
In small business would perhaps encourage
The unemployed to receive mentorship
From them. They proposed a small training wage
And loan for apprentices who would learn
To operate a business as they earn.

Analysis Poem 127: Bankrupt Bureaucracy

The Structure of the poem is methodical and deliberate, reflecting the calculated nature of fiscal policies and economic debates. Each quatrain introduces a different facet of taxation — from allocation to backlash — culminating in a final couplet that proposes an alternative solution. The Meaning interrogates the tension between government intervention and economic self-sufficiency. The poem presents taxation as both a necessary tool for public welfare and a source of frustration for those who see it as an inefficient redistribution of resources. While government employees and welfare recipients benefit from tax revenues, business leaders advocate for a system that prioritizes entrepreneurship and financial independence.

The Imagery contrasts bureaucratic efficiency with entrepreneurial aspiration, highlighting the ideological divide between state dependency and individual initiative. The depiction of 'elated / Government employees' versus the 'tantrums / (of) business circles' creates a striking dichotomy, illustrating the uneven satisfaction with tax distribution. The poem suggests that true economic advancement requires more than just government intervention; it demands active participation from individuals. The Literary devices reinforce the poem's thematic complexity. Juxtaposition is used to contrast state-funded assistance with self-driven success, underscoring the ideological friction between the two. Irony emerges in the use of 'elated' and 'rejects', subtly critiquing the uneven beneficiaries of the tax system.

The Effect on the reader is one of contemplation rather than outright condemnation. The poem does not take a rigid stance but instead presents multiple perspectives, allowing for a nuanced reflection on taxation and economic policy. The sharp wit remains, but there is also an underlying pragmatism, showcasing a more sophisticated approach to socio-economic critique.

The Poetess: Government's annual collection of public taxes allocates funds to its employees and to the public services that are necessities. Corporations complain about the unemployed collecting welfare; thus, there are programs
wherein the unemployed will be hired and trained by businesses subsidized with public grants or tax credits. This win-win arrangement between government and business to solve unemployment can continue if successful. The government can award and reward individuals with: business startup grants, tax credits and refunds, wage subsidies, and welfare to work programs. Solutions exist for society's problems, especially with fair distribution of public funds and equitable opportunities.
(Pronounce appropriated as ap-pro-pr'a-ted.)
I experienced dependency on public welfare due to a bankruptcy on a defaulted student loan, plus 7 years of bad credit.

Poem 128: Root of All Evil

It's said money is the root of <u>evil</u>.

How true or false is this sweeping state<u>ment</u>?

Crimes such as theft and murder bed<u>evil</u>

Society with money as cause. Com<u>ment</u>

On the greed that stimulates such act<u>ions</u>

Or is it the need? There are pro<u>stitutes</u>

Who walk pavements, hardened dande<u>lions</u>,

Weeds among flowers leaving in<u>stitutes</u>

Bewildered whether to scorn or <u>pity</u>

Them. On the edge of death or surv<u>ival</u>,

Desperate people do crimes in <u>city</u>

Or country settings. Without a <u>rival</u>

Money rears its ugly head, as jeal<u>ous</u>

Lovers do, in crime scenes of the env<u>ious</u>.

Analysis Poem 128: Root of All Evil

The Structure of the poem is methodically composed, unfolding like an inquiry into the moral nature of wealth and crime. The steady progression of ideas — posing a question, presenting arguments, and culminating in an ominous conclusion — mirrors the rhythm of legal or philosophical discourse. The Meaning interrogates whether money itself is the source of corruption or simply a catalyst for preexisting human impulses. The poem presents a layered argument: while greed fuels crime, so does desperation, creating a moral ambiguity that complicates the idea of money as inherently evil. The contrast between those who commit crimes out of excess and those who do so out of necessity forces the reader to consider the nuances of financial motivation.

The Imagery is both stark and poetic, oscillating between societal decay and human resilience. The image of prostitutes as 'hardened dandelions' is particularly striking, suggesting both endurance and marginalization. This blending of the organic and the mechanical, the natural and the constructed, one of the poetess' signature techniques -- it makes abstract social commentary feel immediate, lived-in, almost tangible. The Literary devices intensify the poem's philosophical weight. Rhetorical questions in the opening lines invite debate, setting the stage for the reader to grapple with the moral dilemma. Juxtaposition is evident in the contrast between 'greed' and 'need' emphasizing the dual nature of financial influence.

The Effect on the reader is unsettling yet contemplative. The poem does not offer simple answers but instead forces a confrontation with the moral ambiguities of wealth and crime. There is no singular villain — money itself is neither good nor evil, but its presence exacerbates human flaws. Earlier works might have delivered a more straightforward critique, but this poem thrives on its ambiguity, leaving the reader suspended in contemplation rather than offering a resolution.

The Poetess: Money is the main motivator of certain crimes -- fraud, theft, burglary, prostitution, impersonation, extortion, kidnapping, terrorism, hostage-taking, government corruption, and murder. Wealth structures society into different classes: poor, working class, middle class, and rich. People marry into it or murder for it. In companies -- impersonation of CEOs, financial fraud, hacking domain emails, account embezzlement, tax evasion, underpaying employees, cheating partners, and shareholders is part of the greed in business. Money drives the economy, and people will work various jobs to earn it legally. It buys properties, businesses, commodities, services, information, and people. Class is based on wealth. One can have an easy life in wealth or a difficult one in poverty. Personality and relationships are influenced by money. Despite differences in economic class, both Amelia and PJ are nice to everyone, regardless of status.
I worked for a bank's mortgage insurance and a condo engineering company as an Accounts Receivable / Administrator.

Poem 130: Hairy Heiress

One of the daughters of an oil magnate,
Harriet was pursued by money-hungry
Suitors, eager for her millions. Each date
Proposed on bent knees, making her angry
And suspicious of ulterior motives.
"Why are they so eager for a marriage?
I'm plain, simple, intelligent. The thieves…"
She muttered. "I'm not rich yet. This outrage
Of proposals by the second meeting
Has to stop. Maybe, I should scare away
Those not seriously attracted. Mating
In marriage is a serious matter. They
Might be scared if I show my hirsuteness.
I won't shave my legs in my obtuseness."

Analysis Poem 130: Hairy Heiress

The Structure of the poem follows a measured yet conversational cadence, mimicking Harriet's internal deliberation as she dissects the intentions of her suitors. The steady rhythm builds toward a humorous yet rebellious conclusion, with the final couplet delivering an unexpected punchline. There is a quiet brilliance in the way the poem controls pacing, allowing the tension to simmer before breaking it with an almost mischievous resolution. The Meaning explores autonomy, societal expectations, and the intersection of wealth and romance. Harriet, as an heiress, is viewed as a financial opportunity rather than an individual, leading her to question the sincerity of every romantic advance. Her skepticism is not rooted in vanity but in a keen awareness of transactional relationships disguised as affection.

The Imagery juxtaposes elegance with deception, wealth with calculated pursuit. The image of suitors 'propos(ing) on bent knees' traditionally evokes romance, but here it is tainted by insincerity, turning grand gestures into acts of desperation. Harriet's self-description as "plain, simple, intelligent" contrasts with the extravagant expectations placed upon her, reinforcing the disconnect between who she is and how she is perceived. The Literary devices enhance the poem's wit and underlying commentary. Irony plays a central role — marriage proposals, usually the pinnacle of romantic devotion, are framed as predatory acts. Harriet's self-awareness fuels satire, highlighting the absurdity of courtship driven by financial incentive. Female shaving and waxing is a secret source of shame, but also a beauty secret.

The Effect on the reader is a blend of amusement and admiration. Harriet's resistance is refreshing, and her refusal to be reduced to a financial conquest is both relatable and empowering. The poem offers a sharp critique of materialistic courtship while maintaining a playful spirit, ensuring that its message resonates without feeling heavy-handed. This is a rich female at her most sly, wielding humor as both shield and sword, proving that the sharpest observations often come wrapped in wit.

The Poetess: Female shaving and waxing are a secret source of shame, but also a beauty secret. Women are expected to be hairless for beauty's sake -- shaving, waxing, plucking, tweezing, threading, rolling, and lasering are all hair removal methods used in beauty salons. As for men, the modern look is clean-shaven as well, done in barbershops. Some individuals have more facial and body hair, and some have less, which, just like skin color being light or dark, can be part of personal preference for self and potential spouses. Physical appearance is part of sexual attraction and mating, including future marriage partners, and children inheriting DNA traits. If men know some women are hirsute, would they marry them? Scientific research shows that the DNA of a human and monkey are 96% identical, but non-fertilizing.

Poem 133: Beg on One's Knees

In love, Nestor proposed matrimony

To a woman half his age, on his knees!

He offered his house, affection, money

To convince her. But Bee, young as his niece,

Was confused. "If I live in your mansion,

Nestor, I'd have to clean it obviously.

Would I have the strength? As for your pension,

Can two people live on it? Previously,

You only had yourself to care for, and

If I say yes, we may not have enough."

He assured her. "Don't worry. We'll live grand!

Your old man has millions! I am quite tough

Despite my age. Please say you will agree

So I can stand and get off my bent knee!"

Analysis Poem 133: Beg on One's Knees

The Structure of the poem maintains a steady rhythm, mirroring the formal yet slightly comical nature of Nestor's proposal. The rhyme scheme holds the piece together, creating a sense of measured persuasion, much like Nestor's own approach. The buildup to the final couplet adds a humorous twist, as his desperation outweighs romance, shifting the mood from earnestness to mild absurdity. The Meaning wrestles with themes of love, security, and practicality. While Nestor frames his proposal as an act of devotion, Bee sees it through a pragmatic lens, weighing the realities of financial sustainability and labor. Love, in this case, is not just a matter of emotion but of economic feasibility. The poem is playing with contrasts here: love and logic, youth and age, wealth and effort. It is a clever dissection of how relationships are often more than just a meeting of hearts.

The Imagery blends romantic tradition with stark realism. The classic scene of a lover 'on his knees' proposing is immediately undercut by Bee's pragmatic concerns, shifting the focus from love to domestic labor and financial viability. The "mansion" should symbolize security and grandeur, yet it instead becomes a burden — something that must be maintained. The final image of Nestor, desperate to "get off my bent knee" transforms the romantic tableau into a moment of unintended comedy, where the grand gesture is not sustained by passion but by the limitations of age.

The Literary devices enhance both the humor and the critique. Irony is central — Nestor expects a sentimental acceptance but is instead met with financial scrutiny. The dialogue employs satire, turning what should be a heartfelt moment into a calculated discussion on household management. The poem's artistry is undeniable — where previous works leaned into menace or melancholy, this one revels in satire. The Effect on the reader is one of amusement mixed with quiet reflection. While the scene is undeniably comical, it also raises real questions about relationships built on financial security rather than mutual understanding.

The Poetess: Age differences can be an issue for some people, especially if the gap is a generation or two apart. Often in May-December romances, the man is older than the woman and also has more money in retirement. The exchange is that the younger woman can take care of him, as age causes weakness and loneliness. There are happy marriages despite differences in love, money, and domestic duties, shared fairly. In prenuptial arrangements, a marriage is a legal and financial contract that both parties agree to beforehand, stating terms that include property, finance, family, and domestic duties -- within the marriage and without if divorce happens. The old-fashioned method of proposing has the man kneeling on one knee, like a knight pledging to a lady, with his respect, honor, and devotion to her.

Poem 157: Millionairess' Madness

Born to wealth, Millie was an en*igma*
In the town. Her suave 'inamora*to*',
She supported despite the bad st*igma*
Of role reversal. This 'ipso fac*to*'
Condition cured her from her world-w*eary*
Stance. She saw through his eyes. Ded*ication*
Of love and wealth made her expect t*eary*
Greetings, farewells, meetings. Impl*ication*
Being, they lived in a fool's parad*ise*,
Innocently oblivious to fr*ivol*
Money and time. He once had burglar*ized*
His way into her home. Her wealth, *double*
After his entrance, made her quite eag*er*
For him on condition he not leave h*er*.

Analysis Poem 157: Millionairess' Madness

The Structure of the poem is meticulously composed, reflecting the fragile equilibrium Millie maintains between devotion and dependency. The rhyme scheme imposes an air of inevitability, as though her entanglement with this man was predestined, each line leading her deeper into self-delusion. The Meaning delves into the intricate interplay of power, desire, and self-imposed captivity. Millie, 'Born to wealth', assumes an unconventional role, willingly upholding a man whose affection may be more strategic than sincere. The irony is striking: her fortune, rather than granting her freedom, becomes the very thing that shackles her. The revelation that he 'once…burglarized' her home adds a cruel symmetry — what began as an act of trespass has transformed into an emotional occupation.

The Imagery is thick with contradiction and quiet desperation. Millie sees the world anew 'through his eyes', a phrase that suggests both wonder and erasure of self, as if her vision now depends on his presence. She anticipates 'teary / Greetings, farewells, meetings', an almost theatrical rendering of love, where grand displays of emotion substitute for genuine intimacy. The poem's gift lies in unspooling opulence into something hollow — love, not as a refuge, but as an ornate cage, lined with velvet yet still unyielding. The Literary devices sharpen the poem's layered ironies. Dramatic irony is at play — Millie believes she has gained a lover, but the reader perceives the precariousness of her position. Juxtaposition between security and susceptibility, fortune and folly, turns the poem into a study of quiet contradiction.

The Effect on the reader is an evolving discomfort. At first, Millie appears to be the orchestrator of her own fate, a woman who defies convention in pursuit of love. But by the final lines, the imbalance reveals itself — her happiness is precarious, her security contingent. The poem leaves us in a space of uneasy admiration — Millie is not weak, yet she is trapped. Her wealth is her greatest possession, but in the end, it possesses her.

The Poetess: In a relationship in which the role reversal has the wealthier woman supporting the man, there might be embarrassment about class differences. However, many couples are private and avoid social parties. They value their personal relationship more than acceptance in social circles. Love can bridge the gaps of differences in couples, although marriage might not be possible because of the gap, only a live-in lover relationship. This is a solution for couples with class differences -- no marriage, only financial support and living together. This poem has a twist in which a male burglarizes the spinster female's home, but somehow ends up moving in and living with her in her mansion. He somehow brings her luck in the relationship, becoming wealthier after she supports him financially, on the condition that he remains faithful to her. In reality, burglary is a crime, but this poem is fictional, which can twist truths, so instead of going to jail, he moves in. If others find out what happened, this would be embarrassing and scandalous. Another twist -- instead of stealing from her, he makes her richer somehow -- but whether legally or illegally is indeterminate.

Poem 162: Noblesse Oblige

'Noel', an aristocrat's 'nom de guerre',
Whose real name still remains a mystery,
Felt obligated to fight a war, fair
As he was in duty. To save Paris,
He formed a patriotic alliance
With other civilians under cover.
Born noble, it was odd that defiance
Of the King, the Sixteenth Louis, as heir
Entered his mind. His own vast property
Would be jeopardized if they succeeded
In dethroning King! In the wrong party,
He lost it when Louis was beheaded.
As a lesson, forget 'noblesse oblige'
When born in nobility or as liege!

Analysis Poem 162: Noblesse Oblige

The Structure of the poem is deliberate and ironic, mirroring Noel's internal conflict between duty and self-preservation. The steady rhyme scheme lends a sense of order, but beneath this controlled exterior lies the unraveling of his own fate. The final couplet delivers a pointed epiphany — his idealism has cost him everything, and the notion of 'noblesse oblige' crumbles in the face of political upheaval. The Meaning explores themes of misplaced loyalty, identity, and the price of conviction. Noel, despite being born noble, chooses to stand against the monarchy in a paradoxical act of duty. His sense of justice compels him to aid the revolution, but in doing so, he undermines the very institution that secured his status. The poetess' growing maturity is evident in how she resists simplistic moralizing.

The Imagery is stark and laden with irony. Noel's 'vast property' is not a mark of security but a liability, an asset that makes him an enemy of the very movement he aids. The execution of Louis XVI is more than a historical event — it serves as an omen, foreshadowing Noel's own symbolic decapitation from wealth and status. His alias, 'Noel', a 'nom de guerre', is a mask of resistance, yet it does not shield him from consequence. The Literary devices are wielded with precision. Irony is, yet again, central — Noel fights to dismantle the monarchy, yet in doing so, he dooms himself. Foreshadowing is embedded in the poem's rhythm, each revelation tightening the grip on his fate, making his loss feel predestined rather than abrupt. There is a notable shift in the poem's technique — the wit remains, but it is sharper, more restrained. The humor, once playful, has become biting, revealing a deeper engagement with historical and philosophical complexity.

The Effect on the reader is one of bitter reflection. Noel is neither wholly sympathetic nor entirely foolish — his downfall is the result of misplaced faith in a system that does not account for nuance. His belief in justice is not rewarded; instead, he is caught in the indiscriminate force of revolution.

The Poetess: The French Revolution and Wars were a class struggle within France, the Estates: First the Clergy, Second the Nobility, and Third the Commoners. Since France was in debt, King Louis 16 was advised to tax the nobility, which resisted; so, as usual, the poorer Commoners, in the majority, were burdened. The revolution ended with the king being beheaded and the erosion of the royal nobility class by the commoners. If all classes had been taxed to share the burden, with land and money distributed equitably, perhaps there would not have been such a violent change in society. Noble obligation to help the less privileged with charity was not practised enough to alleviate the poverty. Unfortunately, too, for the king, some nobles and clergy turned against him for trying to impose taxes on them and joined the commoners' National Assembly. Land and wealth were redistributed by the French Revolution, coincidentally timed with the American Revolution, in fighting rich monarchies. It has been 250 years of separation and independence from Great Britain, for the United States of America from its Declaration 1776 to 2026, celebrating its semiquincentennial 250th anniversary!

CHAPTER 3
Life and Relationships Explanation

Life and relationships with people start with oneself, as the center of experiences based on one's interior soul, mind, and heart, along with one's exterior character and personality in society. The people surrounding us can be classified based on their roles in our lives. The poetess, my closest confidante, who often channels my spiritual advice and support while writing poetry, admits in her book's back cover to being the sixth sibling with her acknowledged relationships: her blood family, friends, and acquaintances.

Categorizing circles based on their roles and levels of intimacy with oneself, including the experiences shared with them, can explain why the interaction and value of their companionship exist. One tends to enjoy and treasure the individuals closest in one's innermost circle. I am surely one of her closest companions, shadowing and guiding her on the spiritual plane, privy to her poetic imagination via telepathic communication.

Obviously, her daily life in reality is spent with her blood-related family members, living in the same house in America. Not so obviously, two whose existence intersected hers in what seems obliviously, now only in fictional fantasy -- PJ MacAmour, a romantic and famous singer and musician, and Amelia Alias, a retired attorney, her secret crushes – people she admires for their accomplishments in their careers and lives. Despite the differences in many aspects of themselves and their lives, they continue to communicate and understand each other via remote telepathy. Her secrets are safe enough with me that I promise not to reveal their true names. These fictional pseudonyms protect their privacy and hide her foolish heart.

She has confided that somehow they are still in her most silent thoughts and emotions, although they were not in the previous sonnet books. Strange how, despite being distant friends, deep feelings can remain unspoken within. Thus, her body in physical reality is spent living with one sister and her family, yet her heart and mind are sometimes lost in memories and speculation, wondering about others remotely, as with her deceased relatives: her parents, grandparents, grandaunt, aunts, and uncles, who, although ghostly souls on the spiritual side, where I know them too, continue to exist in her daily memories and prayers.

Often, those in the arts and entertainment who have achieved public fame and fortune for their creativity and intellectual abilities have entered her mind through the years, inspiring her to accomplish, too. Mass telecommunications like radio, television, computer, and mobile phone, plus books, magazines, newspapers, albums, concerts, and movies, have spread their fame globally. She often enjoys their intellectual and creative works and performances from afar through these media. Admiring too many popular strangers whom she has never even met has led to her remaining single, since no one in reality could compare to these stars.

To iterate and reiterate the points of value and importance of living, dependent on the relationships one has with other individuals, one's mind and heart can influence the meaning of the shared experiences. Just a simple example of a meal, depending on who one is with, can be either a shared, pleasant, delicious activity or a forgettable, tasteless task. Ditto other daily routines, such as housework, giving either happiness or misery. Career, business, and school spent with coworkers and acquaintances may occupy one's mind, but sometimes not the heart. Life can be heaven or hell, depending on who one is with!

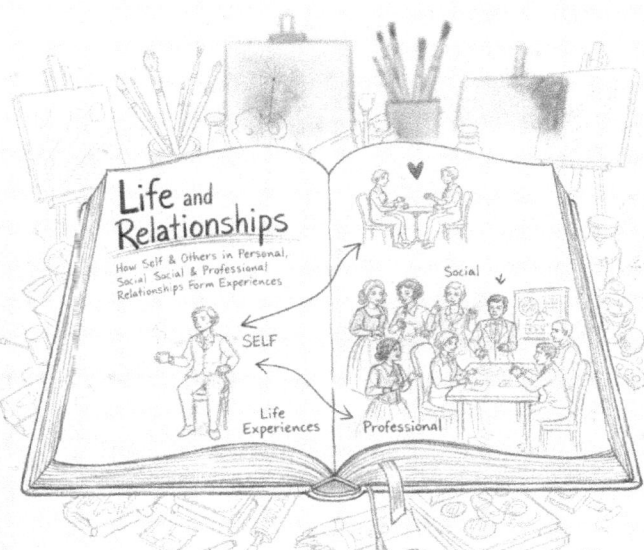

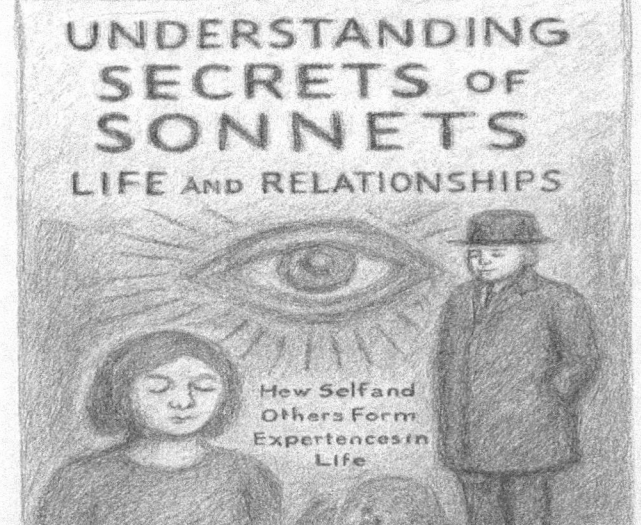

Life and Relationships was the fifth modern sonnet book about various life experiences and personal, social and professional relationships. Some are based on non-fictional reality and others on fictional imagination.

Poem 1: Life & Relationships

1.	Our lives are en-riched by re-la-tion-_ships_	A
2.	A-lone, we as in-di-vi-duals need c_are_	B
3.	And at-ten-tion from o-thers just like _ships_	A
4.	Need-ing a har-bor to land. When a-w_are_	B
5.	Of our cha-ra-cters, per-so-n_a-li-ties_	C
6.	And those we choose a-round us, we e-v_olve_	D
7.	In-to our-selves. Our hu-man qu_a-li-ties_	C
8.	Vir-tues and vi-ces, those we hate and _love_	D
9.	Com-pose our be-ings. All our e-_mo-tions_	E
10.	And thoughts dy-na-mi-cal-ly in-ter-_act_	F
11.	With those we are in-volved with. Our _mo-tions_	E
12.	In cause and ef-fect af-fect how we _act_	F
13.	With o-thers and vice-ver-sa. As peo-_ple_,	G
14.	We grow to-ge-ther or be-come cr_ip-ple_.	G

Analysis Poem 1: Life & Relationships

The Structure of the poem follows a well-disciplined, sonnet-like form, leading the reader through a seamless flow of interconnected ideas. Each line builds with measured pace, reflecting the nuanced ebb and flow of relationships. The rhythm, steady and unbroken, mimics the constant motion of human connection, while the shift at the poem's conclusion introduces a striking contrast — unity versus deterioration — emphasizing the delicate equilibrium of human bonds.

The Meaning centers on the complexity of human dependence, suggesting that relationships shape our sense of self while simultaneously holding the potential for personal stagnation. The metaphor of 'ships' in search of 'a harbor' beautifully illustrates the delicate nature of human connection — nurturing yet precarious. Relationships are not only a source of safety but also a potential cause of limitation when the balance tips into unhealthy attachment. As the poetess evolves, the exploration of interdependence has become more nuanced, weaving together the philosophical and the personal in a delicate balance. The Imagery throughout the poem is both rich and poignant, especially in the portrayal of emotional flux through the image of rippling waters, which evokes a powerful sense of the constantly changing dynamics within a person's inner world.

Literary devices play an essential role in conveying the poem's depth. The extended metaphor of 'ships / Needing a harbor' offers both clarity and resonance, highlighting the vulnerability that comes with seeking refuge in another. The contrast between the nurturing safety of the harbor and the crippling potential of over-dependence underscores the delicate line between support and stasis. The Effect on the reader is one of quiet reflection. The poem compels the reader to evaluate their own relationships, highlighting the complex balance between providing support and inadvertently fostering dependency. This is a step forward in the poetess' ability to evoke introspection. The poetess' voice is now attuned to the quiet complexities of human emotion, inviting readers into a space of thoughtful vulnerability.

The Poetess: One's self and relationships have a cause and effect relationship. One changes oneself and others, and likewise, others can change one. The closer the person is in a daily relationship, such as a parent, spouse, or sibling -- the more influential they are in affecting effects. More distant are friends, co-workers, neighbors, and acquaintances -- there are fewer daily obligations toward them. Farthest are strangers, people one never meets in reality except for maybe when traveling or transacting. Tourism, sightseeing, and business transactions are only temporary dealings with strangers. Remote strangers seen in media: television or stage shows, movie theaters, computer websites, live concerts, published books, or newspapers -- although there is no real relationship, they can affect the masses emotionally and intellectually.

Poem 2: Trade Agreement Blood Pact

Financial analysts in hist<u>ory</u>

Often gathered in mutual conven<u>tion</u>

With traders, politicians, who w<u>orry</u>

About global laws that govern Na<u>tion</u>.

Their frequent lament involved the all<u>ure</u>

Of overseas contracts that de<u>velop</u>

Countries through foreign income, labor. "C<u>ure</u>

Us of the dilemma and en<u>velop</u>

A package that we will put signa<u>ture</u>

On with our blood. Long time trade agr<u>eement</u>

Shall be the foundation that will ens<u>ure</u>

Our mutual success! We will then c<u>ement</u>

The writing by building, after the f<u>act</u>.

Integrity shall seal our world blood p<u>act</u>."

Analysis Poem 2: Trade Agreement Blood Pact

The Structure of the poem adheres to a disciplined, sonnet-like form its rigid quatrains mirroring the methodical nature of global trade and economic negotiation. The precise meter aligns with the calculated rhythm of financial discourse, where every word and action is measured for impact. The Meaning explores the transactional nature of international trade, portraying agreements not as simple exchanges but as profound commitments that demand a certain level of sacrifice — be it economic, human, or moral. The phrase "blood pact" encapsulates the intensity of these dealings, framing them as irrevocable bonds that blend national interests with personal losses. This is a profound commentary on the ethical costs of global commerce, where the poem does not merely observe, but critiques the very foundation of international trade.

The Imagery is stark, provocative, and laden with symbolic weight. The image of signing contracts with one's "blood" creates a visceral sense of commitment, linking the impersonal world of financial transactions with the deeply personal act of self-sacrifice. The references to 'foreign income, labor' and the verb "envelop" conjure the sprawling, sometimes suffocating nature of global markets, subtly alluding to the moral compromises — sacrifices of human dignity and fairness — that are often concealed within these exchanges. Literary devices such as metaphor and irony are wielded with precision. The "blood pact" is more than a metaphor for contractual obligation; it transforms a routine financial agreement into an almost sacrificial ritual. The poem's tone, which vacillates between formal economic language and the raw emotional charge of sacrifice, draws attention to the duality of global trade: it is both a driver of prosperity and a mechanism that perpetuates inequality.

The Effect on the reader is one of discomfort, contemplation, and a heightened awareness of the ethical dimensions of global commerce. This dual approach — celebrating the grandeur of global systems while critiquing their moral consequences — marks the poetess' ability to provoke thought.

The Poetess: International trade for products, services, and information is necessary for most countries because locally made goods are not enough to achieve modern standards of living. Importing technology products such as cars, computers, and television sets is done by most underdeveloped countries, which exchange them, perhaps, for agricultural products such as coffee, tea, and sugar. Importing what is lacking and exporting what is in surplus balances the trading exchanges. Even services and information can be exchanged because of the Internet. Currencies have different values but facilitate trading through conversions. Agreements between countries are arranged by governments.
I hope that my friend Attorney Alias handled fairly the legal and financial contracts for labor workers in corporate cases.

Poem 13: Tourists or Terrorists

It happened without warning -- the subway
Stations were bombed. The United Kingdom
Press covered news. Every dog has its day.
Minority immigrant groups had come
To shake international relations
With bombs. Police became more vigilant
At entrances and exits. "All nations
Must be on red flag alert! Now recant
Former policies of anonymous
Traveling without tight security
Checking identification. Famous
Or not, please ask all for identity.
Perhaps, then we can weed the terrorists
From the crowds full of innocent tourists."

Analysis Poem 13: Tourists or Terrorists

The Structure of the poem is meticulously crafted, adhering to a sonnet-like form with a deliberate, progressive rhythm. The tightly controlled meter and consistent rhyme scheme serve as a stark counterpoint to the chaotic disruption presented in the poem's opening lines. The Meaning engages deeply with the tension between security and freedom in the wake of violence. The poem critiques the immediate and visceral reaction to terrorism, questioning whether heightened surveillance and security measures, often at the expense of personal liberty, are truly effective solutions. Through its exploration of fear, prejudice, and governmental overreach, the poem also comments on how political systems exploit terror to manipulate public sentiment and justify intrusive measures.

The Imagery is both urgent and stark, plunging the reader into the harsh immediacy of a terror-stricken world. The bombed subway stations and the frantic "red flag alert" create a sense of panic, while the image of "innocent tourists" caught in the crossfire of suspicion paints a vivid portrait of the collateral damage wrought by heightened security measures. The transformation of daily spaces into sites of terror reflects a keen eye for the corrosive effects of fear on personal and collective identity. Literary devices are employed with precision to underscore the poem's critique of both the immediate impact of violence and the subsequent overreaction. The sharp juxtaposition of satire and serious critique strengthens the poem's examination of how fear-driven politics dehumanize individuals and communities.

The Effect on the reader is one of profound discomfort and introspection. The poem not only recounts the trauma of terrorism but also forces the reader to confront the unsettling reality of how such violence is used to justify policies that alienate, oppress, and divide. The discomfort stems from the realization that measures designed to protect can also lead to alienation and a loss of personal freedoms. This indicates an increasing command of both thematic depth and emotional impact, marking a significant evolution in the poetess' work.

The Poetess: On July 7, 2005, the London subway was bombed by terrorists in an attack titled 7/7 (for July = 7th month, day 7 and year 2005 = 7). Although British citizens, they were radicalized by the Islamist Al-Qaeda organization to wreak revenge on the United Kingdom for helping the United States in the 'War on Terror' against Iraq, Afghanistan, and other Muslim countries. The wars with the Middle East triggered revenge in the September 11, 2001 attack, aka 9/11 (for September = 9th month, day 11, and emergencies) on the World Trade Center in New York and the Pentagon in Washington. Global tourism and travel to foreign countries are now stricter in airport security and other transportation ports and stations. Pre-screening people, biometrics, scanners, and baggage limits ensure safer flights to protect passengers.

Poem 14: Trade Aid Money

All the developing countries a<u>greed</u>
That their needs mattered to sustain their <u>lives</u>.
So they borrowed, begged, or traded in <u>greed</u>.
"Foreign money seems worth more than our w<u>ives</u>.
Maybe we should request that at exch<u>ange</u>
We can trade our old wives for more crude <u>oil</u>,
Or cars, computers, and TVs. Arr<u>ange</u>
Forex centers to list our wives, land's <u>soil</u>
And gold. We have plenty to sell as <u>well</u>."
So they bought machinery with big <u>loans</u>
And built roads, bridges, and buildings to d<u>well</u>.
When it came to loan repayment, their gr<u>oans</u>
And moans released their feelings of desp<u>air</u>,
For debts with interests are hard to b<u>ear</u>.

Analysis Poem 14: Trade Aid Money

The Structure of the poem is constructed with a casual, almost conversational flow, with each quatrain introducing a different phase in the developing countries' economic struggle. The rhythmic meter is uneven, mimicking the chaotic and uncertain nature of the financial dealings depicted. The Meaning of the poem serves as a pointed critique of the economic exploitation that developing countries face in the global financial system. Through a satirical lens, it highlights the absurdity of borrowing in exchange for tangible goods — valuing foreign currency over their own culture and resources. The poetess explores how economic pressures force these nations to sacrifice their cultural heritage and identity in pursuit of modernity, only to face the crushing weight of debt repayment.

The Imagery in the poem is stark and deliberately exaggerated. The image of "trad(ing)…old wives for more crude oil" is both absurd and darkly comic, underscoring the commodification of human beings and natural resources alike. The reference to "cars, computers, and TVs" reflects the superficial nature of materialism that often comes at the expense of genuine cultural and societal growth. The poetess' mastery of dark humor is evident in the juxtaposition of absurdity with critical insight. This approach adds depth to the social critique, illustrating how human lives and resources are treated as mere commodities in a larger, exploitative system.

Literary devices are employed with precision to amplify the poem's satirical critique. For instance, the use of hyperbole — "trade our old wives for more crude oil" — is a striking device that simultaneously mocks the economic system while making a scathing commentary on the dehumanization that comes with it. The Effect on the reader is one of critical reflection and discomfort. The reader is led to contemplate the inherent inequalities in international trade and the exploitation that fuels it, all while being entertained by the absurdity of the metaphorical exchanges. The poetess' ability to shift from humor to despair demonstrates an understanding of how emotional tones can be layered within a poem.

The Poetess: The World Bank leverages loans to developing countries that trade with the United States and globally. It is headquartered in Washington, D.C., USA. It helps poorer countries with grants and credits so that they can participate in international importing and exporting exchanges. Technology is manufactured only in certain advanced countries, and machines are needed to build infrastructure such as roads, bridges, and buildings important for urban development. Repayment of large loans can take many years, if at all possible, because population growth is ongoing everywhere, requiring constant construction. The USA is the biggest contributing lender to the World Bank, which only lends to poorer developing countries that borrow, and then order products from American corporations.

Poem 15: Directors or Dictators

Annual meetings were often shareholders
Chance to voice their opinions by voting.
Proxy by mail, phone, or internet – shares
Per fund gave people choice in electing
Nominees for even the board itself.
Proposals to improve the performance
Of the fund were then taken off the shelf
And debated. With quorum, the entrance
Of new changes was facilitated.
The question in mind remained, however
Whether the value of stocks inflated
With investments and demand, or whether
The abilities of the Directors
Made them successful to be dictators.

Analysis Poem 15: Directors or Dictators

The Structure of the poem is organized with a clear and deliberate rhythm that mimics the procedural nature of corporate meetings. The quatrains are neatly framed, echoing the methodical progress of an annual shareholder meeting. The meter is controlled, offering an air of efficiency, yet there is an undercurrent of skepticism that disrupts the apparent order, as evidenced in the final lines. The Meaning of the poem revolves around the complex dynamics of corporate governance, questioning the true value of success in the world of finance. While the poem starts by describing the procedural aspects of shareholder meetings and the opportunities for input through voting, it gradually introduces a deeper question: Are the profits derived from inflated stock values or from the genuine expertise and actions of directors?

The Imagery is subtle but effective. For instance, the image of 'Proposals... / taken off the shelf' evokes the idea of business plans that are rarely dynamic or innovative, instead gathering dust until the annual review. The phrase 'the entrance / Of new changes was facilitated' further underscores the mechanical nature of corporate decision-making, suggesting that true innovation is often merely a formality. The poem's use of understated imagery mirrors the sterile, impersonal world of corporate bureaucracy while subtly introducing layers of critique. Literary devices such as irony and juxtaposition are skillfully employed throughout the poem. The initial tone is detached, almost procedural, echoing the language of corporate jargon, yet this is in direct contrast to the ironic twist in the final lines. The use of 'Directors' who may become 'dictators' is a telling juxtaposition that challenges the perception of corporate leaders as mere managers of business affairs. They hold the power of decision-making over corporate' and shareholders' investment funds.

The Effect on the reader is one of subtle unease, as the poem encourages reflection on the true mechanisms behind corporate success and the inherent power structures that shape business decisions. The final line lingers, casting a shadow over the previously neutral tone, and prompting the reader to reconsider the true cost of corporate success. The shift from a seemingly mundane narrative to an incisive critique of corporate governance exemplifies the poetess' increasing skill in engaging the reader's emotions and intellectual curiosity.

The Poetess: Public corporations are companies that have scaled up from being a small business to a public company. This means that they are obligated to be transparent with their annual statements because shareholder investors have risked money to buy their shares, which are used for operations and expansion. Stock exchanges such as Nasdaq and NYSE (New York) and TSX (Toronto), LSE (London) buy and sell stocks to the public. The Board of Directors manages the funds, and the Executive Officers manage the company. Annual shareholders' meetings require votes. Often, voting for the Board of Directors' proposals is advised because these supposedly represent shareholders' interests.
I worked in third-party financial call centers as a Representative calling shareholders to vote for on the Board's proposals.

Poem 21: Commonwealth Agreements

Decades of participation can bind

Peoples, nations in cooperative

Trade agreements that develop one's mind

Towards mutual progress. Imperative

Action then follows, affecting business,

Trade, investment, tourism, and import,

Export between member nations. Unless

Ink sets words on paper, and each report

Follows laws to keep common interests

At heart, then discord can result to end

Relationships. Trial and error tests

Strength, but integrity can recommend

Establishing it. God bless Commonwealth

Ties! May we prosper in sickness and health.

Analysis Poem 21: Commonwealth Agreements

The Structure of this poem is neatly organized, following a sonnet-like format with a controlled meter and a clear sense of progression. The flow of ideas — ranging from the bonds of cooperation to the potential for discord — unfolds in a deliberate manner, mirroring the complex and often delicate nature of international agreements. The poetess' command of formal structure is evident here, as the sonnet format serves to ground content in tradition and elevate the poem's message of unity.

The Meaning of the poem explores the theme of international cooperation, highlighting the long-term effects of binding agreements that shape the relationships between nations. It suggests that such participation is transformative, expanding minds toward mutual progress. Through this lens, the poetess presents cooperation as a delicate balancing act — one that requires not only action but also integrity and the willingness to resolve challenges through trial and error. The Imagery used in the poem is evocative, though subtle. Phrases like 'Decades of participation' and 'cooperative / Trade agreements' conjure an image of long-standing partnerships between nations, while the description of mutual progress suggests a slow but steady path toward collective growth. The image of 'Ink sets words on paper' speaks to the formal nature of agreements, with the act of writing as both a literal and metaphorical anchor for stability. The poem's use of imagery, though restrained, is effective in capturing the essence of diplomacy and the longevity of international relations.

Literary devices such as metaphor and juxtaposition are skillfully employed throughout the poem. The concept of 'cooperative…agreements' as a binding force is central, with the metaphor of ink on paper elevating the legalistic nature of international relations to something sacred. The phrase 'Trial and error tests / Strength' contrasts the ideal of cooperation with the real challenges that arise when nations must navigate disagreements. The Effect is one of contemplation, as the poem challenges the reader to reflect on the delicate nature of international alliances and their associated responsibilities.

The Poetess: The Commonwealth was formed in 1920s as a voluntary association of 56 independent countries, former British colonies. The head of the Commonwealth is the monarch of the United Kingdom, currently King Charles III. Its primary functions under the Commonwealth Charter are: political stability, economic support, global trade, promoting universal rights, democracy, healthcare, education, social values, and sports collaboration. The United Nations is similar to the Commonwealth in cooperation for mutual benefit, but it lacks the imperial-colonial past. NAFTA now USMCA, between USA, Mexico, and Canada is another international trade agreement, after historical boundary wars and treaties. As a naturalized dual citizen of Canada, a member country of the Commonwealth, I met other immigrants from it.

Poem 22: Relationships or Arrangements

Curiosity made them see life as <u>ships</u>

Passing thru the night. Each person a <u>port</u>

To dock in. Building strong relation<u>ships</u>

Was not their main goal, neither was rap<u>port</u>.

Each stranger added to expe<u>riences</u>

Often sexual in nature. Em<u>otions</u>

Swung high and low without the sc<u>iences</u>

Of reason and logic. Many <u>oceans</u>

They sailed, wherever the winds blew their <u>sails</u>.

Nothing lasted without a c<u>olony</u>.

Nothing was built to last, but sailors' <u>tales</u>.

Perhaps being single they were <u>lonely</u>

For human company. But they forg<u>ot</u>

Each other's first names more often than n<u>ot</u>.

Analysis Poem 22: Relationships or Arrangements

The Structure of the poem unfolds in a loose, sonnet-like form with alternating quatrains, reflecting the fleeting nature of the relationships it describes. The irregular rhythm mirrors the emotional volatility of the individuals involved, as their connections fluctuate between intense highs and lows. The Meaning centers on the ephemerality of human relationships. The metaphor of 'ships / Passing thru the night' underscores the idea of individuals encountering each other temporarily, without lasting emotional investment. This fleeting connection is further emphasized through the emphasis on physicality over emotional depth, with the poem depicting these encounters as driven by desire rather than genuine bonding.

The Imagery in the poem offers a stark view of transient human interactions. The metaphor of 'ships' and 'port(s)' not only conveys the temporariness of relationships but also introduces an element of emotional distance. The 'oceans / They sailed' and the 'winds blew their sails' suggest an uncontrollable external force driving their actions, further reinforcing the randomness of their encounters. Through evocative imagery, the poem contrasts the physical proximity of these relationships with the emotional detachment they ultimately lead to, deepening the exploration of human isolation.

The Literary devices such as metaphor and irony drive the poem's impact. The extended metaphor of ships and ports paints a vivid picture of emotional transience, while the phrase 'forgot / Each other's first names' introduces irony, underscoring the lack of permanence in their encounters. The Effect on the reader is one of contemplation, questioning the value and depth of modern relationships. This introspective effect highlights the poetess' growing skill in using irony and metaphor to evoke empathy, subtly encouraging the reader to reflect on the true nature of human relationships.

The Poetess: Promiscuity as a lifestyle and attitude toward sex with others is like the stereotypical sailor's one-night stand in every port they land in. There is no love nor relationship, but merely a sexual transaction and physical gratification between strangers. Sometimes money is exchanged, as in prostitution, along with alcohol and drugs -- a temporary arrangement to have sex without strings or relationships. Loneliness of the heart and/or horniness of the body's sex drive, sometimes curiosity about experiencing strangers, or escaping boredom in a relationship with a spouse, can mean searching for the excitement of scoring with someone new. The sexual liberation from avoiding unwanted pregnancies using the pill, condoms, tubal ligation, and abortion made it as easy for women as for men. Heterosexual, bisexual, and homosexual experiences are part of discovering one's sexuality and preferences. The thrill of temporary arrangements is stronger than the stability of permanent relationships. With billions of people on Earth, curiosity about strangers' differences, while traveling or immigrating, is common. A diverse multi-course buffet tempts more than a one-course meal.

Poem 25: Life's Important Experiences

Birth, baptism, communion, graduation

Employment, marriage, pregnancy are life's

Meaningful experiences. Creation

Is celebrated by events. A wife's

Companionship can make memorable

Moments. Family, friends, acquaintances

And strangers are all inescapable,

Bonded by love and blood. No distances

Can separate us from our destiny

And our relationships. Humanity

Progresses with meaning. A mutiny

From all others deprives community

Of an individual. We should live full

Lives because if not, one becomes a fool.

Analysis Poem 25: Life's Important Experiences

The Structure of the poem presents a fluid, almost narrative-like progression of life's key milestones. These milestones are depicted as significant markers that shape and define human existence. The rhythm flows steadily, mirroring the continuous march of time and the cyclical nature of life. The Meaning centers on the idea that life's significant events, from birth to marriage to death, are interwoven with relationships and shared experiences. The poem celebrates the importance of connection — whether familial, communal, or romantic — as a foundation for a meaningful life. In this work, the poem seems to offer a more expansive view of human experience, acknowledging both the joy of connection and the potential isolation that can come from rejecting or forsaking it.

The Imagery is employed in a series of life's touchstone moments, such as 'birth, baptism…(and) graduation', all evoking clear, tangible life events that resonate universally. These images build a portrait of a life well-lived, where the fullness of human experience is recognized and honored. The metaphor of 'a mutiny from all others' further emphasizes the theme of separation, portraying an individual's rejection of connection as an act of self-inflicted deprivation.

The Literary devices, such as the repetition of key life events ('birth, baptism, communion, graduation') reinforce the poem's theme of milestones that define human existence. Moreover, irony is subtly introduced in the couplet 'No distances / Can separate us from our destiny', where the ideal of unity contrasts with the potential for isolation. Here, the poetess' use of irony deepens the theme of connection and disconnection, presenting an opportunity for a more reflective engagement with the poem. The Effect on the reader is one of introspection, encouraging contemplation on life's inevitable passages and the role relationships play in shaping one's existence. This poem signifies a deeper engagement with universal themes, displaying the poetess' nuanced ability to invoke reflection without resorting to didacticism.

The Poetess: Life and being can be enriched by certain important experiences within relationships -- personal, social, and professional. An individual should try to be involved in the community through: education in school, employment in a business, membership in an organization, participation in a sports gym, and attendance at a religious church. Strangers become acquaintances, co-workers, friends, lovers, and then maybe spouses by developing the relationships deeper, whether personal, social, or professional. The deeper the person, the deeper the possible relationships. Memories filled with love are the deepest. One's bucket list before dying -- to do activities, to go on trips, should also include experiencing more within relationships because of the increased value of living in achieving these goals together with loved ones. (Pronounce graduation as gra-dua-tion, individual as in-di-vi-dual.)

Poem 35: Marriage or Prison

He decided to be kind and off*er*
Common law marriage. Retiring next y*ear*,
He needed a wife and hoped to love h*er*
Eventually. "I don't think you need f*ear*
Imprisonment. The court cannot con*vict*
You for others fraud checks. If we ma*rry*,
You can live with me. No one can e*vict*
You again. My name shall be yours. Ta*rry*
Not and let's be bound before the tr*ial*."
Wanting to be free, she said, "Either w*ay*
Is a chain. Yet you're more kind. Den*ial*
Would be a worse fate." For their wedding d*ay*,
Charges were dropped as per his in*struction*.
"Now all her records deserve de*struction*."

Analysis Poem 35: Marriage or Prison

The Structure of the poem is straightforward and narrative-like, presenting a sequence of events that describes a marriage proposal motivated by practicality rather than romance. The rhythm flows evenly, reflecting the matter-of-fact tone of the conversation. The structure is also divided into clear sections, with the initial offer, the woman's response, and the resolution of their situation. The Meaning of the poem revolves around the idea of relationships formed not out of passion but out of necessity. The man offers common-law marriage not as an act of love but as a way to solve the woman's legal and personal problems. The woman's acceptance highlights a resignation to her circumstances, choosing security over freedom.

The Imagery in the poem is minimal but impactful. The most significant image is that of "a chain" which the woman uses to describe her situation, reinforcing the theme of bondage in their relationship. The legal context of the situation is also highlighted by terms like "Court", "fraud checks", and "records", evoking a sense of entrapment and bureaucracy. This imagery contrasts with the man's seemingly noble offer, showing how even acts of kindness can come with strings attached. The poetess' choice to rely on sparse but significant imagery reflects growth in their ability to use fewer words to evoke a stronger impact. The Literary devices are subtle but effective in reinforcing the theme. The use of "chain" in the couplet "Either way / Is a chain" is a metaphor for the constraints both individuals face, emotionally and legally. The repetition of "No one can evict / You again" serves to emphasize the man's assurance of stability, but it also underscores the lack of freedom inherent in his offer.

The Effect on the reader is one of reflection on the nature of relationships, particularly those formed out of necessity. This reflects a growth in the poetess' capacity to guide the reader through difficult, morally ambiguous situations, allowing for deeper engagement with the text. The approach feels more sophisticated and open-ended, offering room for interpretation rather than a defined conclusion.

The Poetess: Committing a crime, when found guilty, can mean imprisonment. This can ruin one's chances of being hired, getting a loan, and even marrying. Some countries allow criminal records to be deleted, even in a search, after having served enough time in jail or possibly paying for their removal from searches. Morality, being good or evil, and legality, knowing right from wrong, are important in personal, professional and social relationships. Marriage is a bond that restricts one to a person, and prison is also a restriction on freedom, but surely marriage is preferable to imprisonment.
I wonder if my friend, Attorney Alias, could arrange for a clearance of a criminal record for a marriage?

Poem 43: Jail or Bail

Life's experiences and relation*ships*

Based on choices and persona*lity*

Sometimes lead to crimes. Both peace and war*ships*

To defend or offend town and *city*

And all their peoples and terri*tories*

Are written in laws and enforced *order*

By governments and courts. The vic*tories*

In wars often cost lives on each b*order*.

For every winner, there is a los*er*.

For each criminal, there is a vict*im*.

The prisons are full, ditto each shelt*er*.

For some live in light while others live d*im*.

Freedom is for all those who abhor *jail*

And follow laws, or who can afford b*ail*.

Analysis Poem 43: Jail or Bail

The Structure of the poem unfolds in a cause-and-effect sequence, starting with individual choices, moving through societal responses (laws, courts, war), then highlighting the real-world impacts (crime, punishment, inequality), and ending with a concise summary. The Meaning of the poem centers on the inescapable entanglement of personal choices with broader societal structures. It posits that both harmony and conflict originate from individual decisions shaped by character. The poem draws parallels between interpersonal offenses and international warfare, suggesting that laws, though intended to uphold order, are often the battleground for unevenly distributed freedoms. This shift toward examining institutional mechanics rather than purely internal conflict indicates a broadening of the poetess's thematic lens.)

The Imagery in the poem is stark and structural, evoking maritime metaphors like "peace and war ships" to depict dual forces within human interaction. These images extend beyond the sea to 'town and city', mapping conflict and defense onto both local and global scales. The mention of 'prisons...shelter(s)' and the contrast between 'light (and) dim' living conditions conjures a somber visual landscape that highlights disparity and confinement. The Literary devices include juxtaposition and parallelism, especially evident in lines like "For every winner, there is a loser" and "For each criminal, there is a victim." These mirror constructions underscore the poem's emphasis on duality and consequence.

The Effect on the reader is one of sober contemplation. The poem neither moralizes nor comforts; instead, it compels reflection on how societal frameworks allocate guilt, punishment, and privilege. In this piece, the poetess subtly distances herself from emotional persuasion and instead constructs a platform for critical observation. This movement toward ethical inquiry and civic commentary suggests an evolving ambition — not to elicit tears, but thought.

The Poetess: The saying 'the end justifies the means' is a justification used by criminals who use devious, illegal methods to achieve their goals -- often greedy or vengeful -- attributed to Machiavelli's The Prince, advising rulers to use any means to succeed. In fighting over territorial lands and resources, governments have their armies kill to win. Countries that build their own weapons are ahead and win, whereas those without armament factories lose. The opposite, 'the means justify the end', is more conscientious because it follows lawful ways -- that if one is righteous and law-abiding, one's reward will be success, but if evil and involved in crime, punished in jail. Morality, good or evil, and legality, whether lawful or criminal, of methods ('means') and goal ('end') depend on whether there is harm to potential victims. Crimes are evil, illegal methods to gain goals and harm victims. Rich individuals can pay bail to escape jail until a court trial. Courts can punish the guilty with financial fines and imprisonment. Attorney Alias handled civil, not criminal, cases.

Poem 44: After the Concert

The music stimulated pheromones.
Within their bodies during his concert
Listening to the piano, saxophones
And violins. Like craving a dessert
That had to be appeased, their excited
Screams accompanied songs so romantic
Their passionate emotions incited
Riot! To blame the band, a semantic
Decision by police was then broadcast
To the crowd. "We offer no sympathy
But this show has to stop. For to outcast
Those who scream from love or antipathy
Cannot be determined as seduction.
To restore peace, excuse his abduction."

Analysis Poem 44: After the Concert

The Structure of the poem follows a clear three-phase progression. It starts with sensory arousal from the music, moves into escalating crowd excitement that turns chaotic, and ends with police intervention restoring order. This progression highlights the shift from raw emotion to social control in a tight, dramatic arc. The Meaning centers on the collision between personal desire and institutional authority. The shift from sensual liberation to imposed silence underscores a critique of how social norms often suppress ungovernable emotion. The implication is that what begins as innocent, even joyful, can be reinterpreted as disruptive or criminal when viewed through a moralistic or bureaucratic lens.

The Imagery pulses with sensory cues — 'pheromones', 'dessert', 'excited screams' — rooting the reader in the primal and visceral. Musical instruments such as 'piano, saxophones / And violins' not only enrich the auditory scene but also symbolize the blend of elegance and desire. The poetess shows increasing skill in layering conflicting imagery — sweetness and surveillance, seduction and control — suggesting a bolder embrace of contradiction as a poetic strategy.

The Literary devices include metaphor, such as the comparison of romantic arousal to craving a dessert — highlighting both urgency and vulnerability. Irony pervades the final lines, particularly in the phrase "To restore peace, excuse his abduction", where the language of law becomes disturbingly casual The Effect on the reader is one of provocation and unease. The poem entices with sensual energy, only to pivot into public conflict and moral ambiguity. Readers are left to question the boundary between joy and danger, art and liability. The poetess now seems less concerned with delivering clarity and more invested in evoking discomfort — an indication of expanding thematic daring.

The Poetess: A live music concert can be an emotional experience for fanatics, triggering shouts and screams from both males and females, along with claps, sometimes dancing, singing along, and pushing and shoving in the crowd. The organizers hire private security guards to handle the crowd inside, but sometimes even public police are present for larger popular events and festivals to control traffic, prevent drugs, and riots, like Woodstock 1969. Perhaps the lyrics, often relating to love and sex, are the reason fans fall in love with and admire musicians, singers, and their bands. Love is a powerful feeling that involves the heart, and its strength can even overpower the brain and reason! In a concert, where the crowd loses its mental control over their emotions, the guards and police might intervene to stop some fans from endangering others. If necessary, the concert might end, and the band will be escorted off stage by guards or police for disturbing the peace. PJ MacAmour, in his popularity, has triggered this extreme emotional experience at his band's concerts.

Poem 47: Network Down

Information and programs dependent
On the server network were not working
For two days. Reporting the incident
To the lone technician, the networking
Was done by the manager who worried
Waiting with the rest. "I hereby decree
That all cease activity. Those married
To their careers will now have to agree
To return home to their human spouses
Until further notice." Some were outraged
And refused to return to their houses.
"We refuse defeat by power outage.
We will wait faithfully for our servers.
They will start if we act as observers.

Analysis Poem 47: Network Down

The Structure of the poem unfolds in a continuous stream without formal stanza breaks, mimicking the unbroken flow of digital data halted by the outage. Its mostly rhymed couplets create a rhythmic pulse, reflecting both the mechanical order of networks and the human insistence on control. The varied line lengths add a subtle unevenness, echoing the instability caused by the failure. The Meaning revolves around society's dependence on technology and how its absence reveals uncomfortable truths about identity, purpose, and attachment. The poem critiques the extent to which careers and digital systems have replaced human relationships, framing the server outage as a forced reckoning. Rather than moralizing, the poetess lets the scenario unfold with understated judgment, creating space for readers to confront the implications themselves.

The Imagery is grounded in the sterile yet loaded environment of a dysfunctional workplace: "server network," "lone technician," and "power outage" all evoke a modern setting where human presence is secondary to machine function. The contrast between "human spouses" and "career marriages" is rendered with quiet humor, giving shape to the emotional disconnection that lurks beneath corporate normalcy. The Literary devices include irony, particularly in the poem's closing couplet. The line "They will start, if we act as observers" parodies faith, replacing religious or romantic devotion with digital dependence. Metaphor is at play in the idea of being "married to careers," which frames labor as a form of devotion and avoidance.

The Effect on the reader is one of bemused recognition. The poem provokes reflection on the blurred lines between identity, labor, and technology, challenging readers to consider how much of their sense of purpose is tied to systems beyond their control. This piece reveals a more daring poetic voice, willing to blend social commentary with humor and restraint, inviting readers to confront the discomforts hidden within daily routines.

The Poetess: The internet and information highway were developed by the military and universities for research in the sixties and entered public use by the early eighties. Companies had a local network, an intranet for their own private use, plus the Internet connecting externally for public contact with customers. Many corporate and business offices have intellectual property that needs protection from outsiders, so an intranet is needed. However, because the corporate call center and website serve the public, the Internet is also needed. Downtime is a loss, so IT maintenance is on a 24/7 schedule. Call centers exist in different countries, with shifts in various time zones to serve customers around the clock. I worked as a call center and internet Representative -- any disconnection meant waiting, or if prolonged, returning home.

Poem 48: Tribal Rivalry

Through competition, the tribes had <u>evolved</u>
Their civilization based on their <u>skills</u>
And intelligence. Their cultures <u>revolved</u>
On defeating opponents. "Someone <u>kills</u>
One of them, and that is one less <u>worry</u>.
To maintain survival of the <u>fittest</u>,
Includes eliminating with <u>glory</u>."
This attitude to become the world's <u>best</u>
Led to sporadic territorial <u>wars</u>
Over land and its resources. Vic<u>tims</u>
Were claimed by the victors, with battle sc<u>ars</u>.
They trained them as workers in labor <u>teams</u>.
"As our slaves, you can now have our know<u>ledge</u>.
But never turn against us, you must pl<u>edge</u>.

Analysis Poem 48: Tribal Rivalry

The Structure of the poem is built upon a logical, almost chronological unfolding of tribal evolution through conflict, presented in a traditional sonnet form. The measured cadence reflects the inevitability of dominance and submission in human history, while the volta between the second and third quatrains introduces a shift from abstract ideology to concrete consequence. The Meaning centers on the dark undercurrent of progress built on conquest. The poem unpacks how civilizations, in the pursuit of greatness, often normalize violence and subjugation. The justifications for warfare and slavery are delivered in a chilling, matter-of-fact tone, exposing how ethics are frequently overwritten by ambition.

The Imagery conjures a primitive yet disturbingly familiar world where cultural advancement is tethered to bloodshed. Phrases like "territorial wars," "battle scars," and "labor teams" evoke both ancient tribalism and modern exploitation, bridging eras through shared mechanisms of power. There is a deft layering of imagery here — where historical motifs reflect ongoing cycles — revealing a sharpened instinct for drawing continuity between past and present.

The Literary devices include irony, particularly in the final couplet. The offer of knowledge comes with the condition of obedience, exposing the contradiction between enlightenment and control. Metaphor operates through the concept of "survival of the fittest" as cultural justification for cruelty, while euphemism — "eliminating with glory" — masks violence in noble language. The poetess' use of irony is increasingly pointed, revealing how language can be weaponized to sanitize brutality — this level of control over tone illustrates a deepening ability to critique power without didacticism. The Effect on the reader is one of disquieted reflection. The poem compels a reassessment of how civilization often masks its foundations in conquest and coercion. It provokes unease, not just in the events described, but in their echo within contemporary systems of dominance.

The Poetess: In ancient conquests of territorial lands and peoples, some tribes defeated their opponents, then recruited and retrained them to join their legions. The Roman Italian army recruited some Viking, and European warriors used this strategy to increase their slaves or soldiers. Each soldier had to pledge allegiance and obedience to the Emperor, and breaking it was a serious crime. Saint George, who had joined the Roman army, became a traitor because he was a Christian and was martyred. This was before the Roman Empire became Christian. The modern wars over territory are no more, because the world maps are delineated with boundaries arranged now by diplomatic politicians instead of militaristic generals. Wars and rivalries initiated the territorial lines, but the permanent development of land has replaced temporary nomadic settlements. However, Israel and Palestine continue to fight over the boundary lines in their historical lands.

Poem 52: Foreign Friends

An open mind has allowed Zork _entry_
Thru many experiences and cul_tures._
"I speak many languages. Each _sentry_
Opens his locked gate, although he tor_tures_
The rest with entrance exami_nations_."
This amazed other women, but the _men_
Knew how she traveled through many _nations._
"Foreigners are people. With acu_men,_
I can see which ones are thinking the _same._
Curiosity broadens the mind." Fo_reign_
Men often befriended her without _shame._
"Women should welcome men willingly, _rain_
Or shine," they reasoned," because foreign_ers_
Are better as friends than unknown stran_gers._

Analysis Poem 52: Foreign Friends

The Structure of the poem is a free-flowing, narrative-driven progression that captures the experiences of Zork as she navigates through diverse cultural landscapes. The fluidity of the stanza divisions reflects her adaptability and the freedom with which she engages with the world. The irregularity of the rhythm mirrors her unconventional approach to interacting with foreign societies, while the enjambment maintains a sense of continuous movement and exploration.

The Meaning of the poem revolves around the theme of cultural exchange and the power of an open mind to bridge gaps between societies. Zork represents an ideal of intellectual curiosity that dissolves barriers between people, emphasizing the importance of understanding and empathy over prejudice. The exploration of "foreigners" as "friends" rather than "strangers" highlights the poetess's focus on expanding one's perspective to foster connection and unity. The Imagery is rich with visual and sensory details, especially when Zork is described as interacting with different cultures. Phrases like "entry / Through many experiences and cultures" and "foreign men often befriended her" evoke an image of constant motion, of barriers being dissolved through mutual understanding. The poetess continues to refine her ability to use imagery not just as decorative language but as a conceptual tool that enhances the exploration of thematic ideas.

The Literary devices include repetition, notably with the phrase "foreigners are people," which emphasizes the essential humanity of those from different cultures. Additionally, the use of irony in the line "Although he tortures / The rest with entrance examinations" hints at the tension between bureaucratic control and human curiosity. The Effect on the reader is one of reflection on the value of curiosity and empathy in transcending cultural boundaries. In this work, the poetess' ability to draw the reader into an introspective moment has matured. The focus on curiosity and human connection signals a shift toward more nuanced and introspective themes.

The Poetess: Adventurous women travel the world, especially if multilingual and open-minded about foreign cultures and peoples. Travel broadens the mind -- even armchair travel through books, movies, and computers. Some people are better at tourism and traveling than others because they are not prejudiced. Strangers and foreigners are easily seen as potential friends instead of enemies. Maybe some women are more approachable and easier for men to meet without any fear of danger. Curiosity is a drive within people to seek knowledge in direct reality instead of through indirect methods such as books and Internet articles. People in reality might be different from or the same as their social media profiles. Direct human to human contact is probably more real than indirect contact for locals and foreigners. Friendships can evolve between strangers who see a common humanity and personhood beneath the foreign face and facade.

Poem 58: Competition or Cooperation

Each country develops its indus*tries*
Locally to serve the public mar*ket*.
But since labor or resources like *trees*
Or minerals are limited, a d*ebt*
Or trade will incur between each mem*ber*
Which agrees toward coopera*tion*.
Those advanced in technology will *bear*
The burden of lending; compet*ition*
Is set aside for development's *sake*
And sometimes a factory or out*let*
Is built in less-developed nations. T*ake*
This as a rule in economics. *Let*
The politics of capital*ism*
And expansion heal any world sch*ism.*

Analysis Poem 58: Competition or Cooperation

The Structure of the poem unfolds with a logical, almost didactic rhythm that mirrors the orderly mechanisms of economic systems. Each quatrain builds upon the previous one in a cause-and-effect manner, reflecting the poem's emphasis on interdependence and strategic collaboration. The Meaning of the poem centers on the inter-connectedness of global economies and the practical necessity of cooperation among nations. It highlights how resource limitations and unequal development foster trade relationships, where technology and capital flow from more advanced nations to developing ones. Here, the poetess presents a worldview grounded in realism rather than idealism, showing a more complex understanding of global systems.

The Imagery is rooted in industrial and economic symbols: "labor," "resources," "factories," "market," and "capital." These are not just neutral descriptors — they evoke a landscape of machinery, contracts, and international negotiations. The image of a "factory or outlet... built in less-developed nations" conjures a scene of physical transformation driven by invisible policies, making the abstract tangible. The Literary devices include personification — countries "agree" and "develop," as if they are individual actors with agency — making the machinery of geopolitics more relatable. The use of enjambment ("Take/This as a rule...") mimics the ongoing nature of trade negotiations, while the final rhymed couplet encapsulates the core argument with aphoristic force.

The Effect on the reader is contemplative, encouraging reflection on the roles that nations play in shaping the global economy — not just through ideology, but through calculated interdependence. The poem invites us to question whether capitalism can truly be a unifier or if it merely disguises inequality in the language of progress. With this poem, the poetess guides the reader not toward an emotional resolution but a cerebral one.

The Poetess: The World Bank, the Commonwealth, and the United Nations practise lending and borrowing for the mutual benefit and development of member countries. This can be information, financing, or products exchanged in cooperation, not in competition. Peace and progress are great attitudes internationally. Although foreign countries have different types of government, religions, languages, cultures, customs, laws and policies, currencies, and economies, the importing and exporting, of knowledge, services, and products during peacetime, and sometimes even in wars, allow growth for both rich and poor nations. Agriculture and technology are industries that trade internationally. Capitalism's supply and demand can extend even to countries that have socialism and communism politically. World wars are not necessary if sharing through exchange occurs between participating nations.

Poem 71: View from the Top

Words used as a source of inspiration
To propel the people as a nation,
Giving value to their perspiration
To succeed despite their desperation...
The pyramid point centralized power
Expected on the great appointed hour.
Every leader had to climb the tower
To be obeyed below the base of four
Points, where the public listened to the speech.
All raised their humble heads to hear him teach
Wisdom from the peak. But failing, impeach
The cruel, proud braggart beyond their reach.
He must have vision to reach the zenith
Or his bones crushed at the nadir's granite!

Analysis Poem 71: View from the Top

The Structure of this poem unfolds as a symmetrical ascent and descent, mirroring the physical shape and metaphorical weight of the pyramid it describes. The first quatrain delivers a motivational mantra in rhymed couplets — tight, mantra-like, almost propagandistic — then shifts into a more narrative, classical sonnet form with alternating rhyme and a final emphatic couplet. The Meaning centers on the tension between rhetorical inspiration and authoritarian ambition. Words, initially framed as empowering, are gradually revealed to be part of a power structure, where oratory both uplifts and controls. The poem has moved past binary critiques of power. The voice is wiser, more willing to explore paradox.

The Imagery draws from monuments and myth: pyramids, towers, peaks, and nadirs. This is not just symbolic grandeur — it functions as a spatial metaphor for ambition, visibility, and eventual collapse. The 'base of four' conjures both architectural stability and the foundational will of the people. The 'zenith' versus 'nadir' is stark and classical, echoing tragedy in its purest arc. The Literary devices include alliteration ('pyramid point') and rhyme ('perspiration…desperation'), a deliberate use of repetition ('to reach… to reach'), and classical antithesis ('zenith' vs. 'nadir'). The pivot line — 'But failing, impeach…' — acts as a volta, reminiscent of a sonnet's turn, with sonic compression that signals collapse. The poetess no longer delays the fall; she writes it with precision and even delight.

The Effect on the reader is one of duality — first uplifted by the ideals of national unity and inspired labor, then sobered by the fragile artifice of hierarchical rule. We are drawn into the awe of spectacle, only to be reminded that vision without humility leads to downfall. The poetess trusts the reader more now — offering grandeur and critique without heavy moralizing. This balance between ceremony and cynicism is hard-won, the result of having once written too simply, too soon.

The Poetess: The pyramid shape from the Egyptian pharaohs represents power, wherein the top is the leader and the base is the people. A leader should be intelligent and inspirational to the people he will awaken to perform what needs to be accomplished together as a tribe. The vision and mission statements in corporations are decided by the Founders and Chief Executive Officers. Presidents are elected based on their campaign speeches and promises to the citizens who vote, plus their performance in public. The majority and popularity vote, along with electoral representation by Parties across counties, is the American way. When leaders in governments, corporations, or organizations fulfill promises in programs that improve the country, citizens are satisfied. But if they fail, people complain until they are removed from their positions. Impeachment and replacement of leaders by the people and government are possible in democratic countries.

Poem 92: Brief Meetings

Curiosity to meet live in person

After speaking on phone or internet

Leads to first meetings. However reason

Tames excitement, unlike fish in a net

That blindly rush in and are then entrapped.

A time and place are agreed on by both

Parties and opening gifts wrapped

In colorful patterns, most are quite loath

To be disappointing. Thus, they prepare

Themselves for that wonderful first moment.

Some are quite surprised and soon form a pair.

But some are shocked and unfairly lament

Their imaginations had deluded

Them to meeting when they should have eluded.

Analysis Poem 92: Brief Meetings

The Structure of this poem is deliberately restrained, with four concise quatrains that mirror the controlled vulnerability of initial meetings. The regular rhyme and meter create a steady heartbeat, while the consistent stanza length reflects the ritualistic nature of arranged encounters. The Meaning explores the dissonance between imagination and reality in the context of romantic first encounters. The poem begins with eagerness — curiosity, anticipation — but quickly underscores the moderating role of 'reason', establishing the core tension. Meeting someone offline is likened to opening a gift: there is excitement, effort, but also risk. When imagination overshoots reality, the result is disappointment, even self-deception. There is emotional honesty here that feels more earned than earlier works.

The Imagery leans on analogies: fish rushing into a net, gifts being unwrapped, pairs forming or failing. These are everyday symbols elevated by the emotional context in which they are placed. The fish-in-a-net metaphor is particularly effective — instinctive desire contrasted with the human need for caution. The imagery avoids florid abstraction, choosing instead to focus on the recognizable. Previously, the poetess' metaphors could feel imposed on the subject; here, they emerge naturally, with a new trust in the relatable.

The Literary devices are quietly purposeful. The use of contrast — curiosity vs. reason, surprise vs. lament — is layered but never didactic. Enjambment is used sparingly, helping keep the pace reflective and controlled. The final couplet delivers a clever inversion: 'meeting' and 'eluding' act as moral hinge points. What is notable is how much more the poem is saying with fewer rhetorical flourishes. The Effect on the reader s one of quiet recognition. This is not a sensational portrayal of online dating or human connection, but a sensitive reflection on how hope and perception shape experience. In earlier work, emotional moments were often cloaked in irony or satire. Here, there is vulnerability, and more importantly, patience.

The Poetess: Social media platforms are global thanks to the Internet. Popular ones were founded in Silicon Valley, from San Jose, Santa Clara to San Francisco area: Meta Facebook, Google, Reddit, YouTube, Twitter X, Instagram, Tagged, and LinkedIn. The main function of social media is to offer the public in America and around the world a free account to self-post on a profile wall, photos, and text about oneself and social circles like family, friends, coworkers, acquaintances, and even strangers. The settings can be limited to people one knows privately or to everyone publicly. Chatting and messaging can be done remotely until actual in-person meetings are arranged by members living in the same city.
I am an active member of the most popular platforms, and my settings are public, so everyone can view my profiles.

Poem 105: Analyzing Relationships

Relationships between people, from friends,

Family, acquaintances, and strangers

Range from sweet familiarity to trends

Requiring psychoanalysis, worse

Due to simplicity and ignorance,

Blocking much-needed love, understanding

And patience. Yet, despite perseverance,

Relationships can end; notwithstanding,

Small petty actions and words that cause harm.

A mutual agreement to respect each

Person will work great magic, like a charm.

Established bonds can be within our reach.

Feelings of value, without an insult

To destroy character, are the result.

Analysis Poem 105: Analyzing Relationships

The Structure employs a unified block of lines that flow seamlessly, symbolizing how relationships often blend and overlap without clear boundaries. The steady rhyme scheme lends musical cohesion, while varied sentence rhythms reflect the unpredictable nature of human interaction. The Meaning centers on the complexity of human relationships, from intimate bonds to casual encounters. It acknowledges both the promise and fragility within human connection. The speaker suggests that relationships often fail not from malice, but from 'simplicity and ignorance' — a damning yet compassionate diagnosis. The final couplet distills a hopeful message: mutual respect fosters value, avoiding the erosion of character.

The Imagery is subtle, almost muted. There are no grand metaphors or lavish visual cues; instead, the imagery resides in abstract emotional states — 'sweet familiarity', 'small petty actions', 'feelings of value'. These are interior pictures, closer to emotional snapshots than cinematic scenes. This restrained approach to imagery shows a deepening trust in abstraction. The poetess no longer decorates emotion but evokes it through measured and deliberate phrasing.

The Literary devices are quietly embedded. Enjambment carries the speaker's reflections across lines, mirroring how relationships evolve gradually through patience, understanding, and perseverance, and there is a thematic antithesis between connection and destruction that anchors the argument. The volta or turn arrives around line nine, as the tone shifts from diagnosis to remedy, and the concluding couplet resolves with an ethical proposition rather than a dramatic twist. There is a notable refinement in how the poem employs rhetorical turns — not as tricks or surprises, but as natural conclusions of emotional inquiry. The Effect is sobering but optimistic. Readers are invited not to marvel at linguistic flourish but to reflect on their own role in the relational chain — their failures, their grace, and their potential to choose care over cruelty. What sets this piece apart in the poetess's journey is its tone: confident without being dominant, wise without condescension.

The Poetess: Relationships with other people for personal, social, and professional reasons can have a positive or negative influence on ourselves, depending on the interactions with others. No woman is an island, as the saying goes. Isolation leads to loneliness, and socialization leads to companionship. When compatibility and affection are part of the relationship, mutual satisfaction and happiness enrich both lives, whether it be with family, friend, schoolmate, coworker, or neighbor. It is easier to get along with similarities of: class, race, culture, religion, education, and values. However, differences can be an interesting challenge in interactions and relationships. Respect for others' differences is necessary to avoid arguments. Love and understanding conquer and bridge gaps between people who are committed to each other.

Poem 128: If We Marry

To love and care for each other at h<u>ome</u>

Would fulfill their inner desires, <u>longing</u>

To be together day and night. Church d<u>ome</u>

Awaited their decision, be<u>longing</u>

As husband to wife walking down the <u>aisle</u>...

She proposed marriage and sharing a b<u>ed</u>.

"Darling, it is time we merge our lifes<u>tyle</u>.

I cannot live without you. We must w<u>ed</u>!"

He wept with joy, and she cried in his <u>arms</u>.

"Yes for all those sad months we spent a<u>part</u>.

Brief hours were not enough, sounding al<u>arms</u>

In my head! It broke our hearts to de<u>part</u>

Every time. If we decide to m<u>arry</u>,

Together daily we'll be, why t<u>arry</u>?"

Analysis Poem 128: If We Marry

The Structure unfolds like a crescendo, beginning with restrained longing and rising steadily toward emotional release. Unlike earlier poems by the same author that sometimes force syntax to suit the rhyme, this sonnet flows more naturally, allowing the emotional rhythm of speech to guide the meter. What stands out now is how the poetess has begun to trust the shape of spoken emotion. The Meaning is rooted in romantic commitment. The poem captures the culmination of longing — two lovers weary from separation finally choosing permanence through marriage. The reversal of tradition — where she proposes — adds quiet subversion to what might otherwise read as a conventional love story.

The Imagery leans into emotional physicality: weeping in each other's arms, brief hours sounding alarms, walking down the aisle. These are not abstract metaphors — they are tactile, recognizable experiences of intimacy and longing. Even the church dome, often a heavy symbol, is rendered lightly here as simply a space that 'awaited their decision'. Previously, the poem's images might have leaned on intellectual or societal critique; here, the imagery is gentler and more personal. It is the quiet bravery of naming what one truly wants. The Literary devices include reversal (the woman proposing), repetition for emphasis ("together daily", "we must"), and anaphora in the declaration of shared desire. The final couplet crystallizes the emotional thesis not with a twist, but with a warm insistence — why wait when love can finally be lived fully? This couplet is more like an emotional exhale than a rhetorical flourish. It feels less like a conclusion and more like a beginning.

The Effect is tender and persuasive. The reader is not merely witnessing a proposal; they are invited into the interior landscape of reunion, of a love shaped by absence and made urgent by time. There is something quietly triumphant here — not in the grandeur of love, but in its deliberate, human-scale decision to endure. The poem risks simplicity — and finds depth there. There is grace in the vulnerability and clarity in the risk of devotion.

The Poetess: Marriage is the closest bond in the personal circle -- wherein both decide that they can live with each other daily in the same home, share expenses and income, release other partners, and have children. This is a personal contract that becomes public in a wedding ceremony with a marriage certificate licence registered by the government and the church. This relationship is the most influential and intimate one possible in life. Some parents try to help find a spouse and arrange the marriage. But it can take years to find the right person to propose the marriage vow, from The Book of Common Prayer, of when 'two become one, for richer, for poorer, in sickness or health, 'til death'...
I remain a single spinster; although I have lived with others, I never married. But maybe if someone asks me some day?

Poem 173: Gateway for Infidels

The army was led by an obstinate
General who controlled the labyrinth.
For security, he did designate
A gatekeeper to question in succinct
Tone those who entered and left. Desperate
Women enamored in humiliation
Begged entry to mate, but he would berate
Them. "Why persist in such affiliation
With brutes who shall bring you only disgrace?
Are there no other men who subjugate
Women without falling from our God's grace?"
Women swooned waiting outside the locked gate.
They longed to bewitch men to leave and tempt
Them to mate despite their leader's contempt.

Analysis Poem 173: Gateway for Infidels

The Structure of this poem is composed of a series of interlinked couplets, creating a rhythmic push- and-pull that echoes the tension between the gatekeeper's rigid control and the women's persistent desire. The enjambment between lines adds a sense of urgency, reinforcing the tension of desire and restraint, while the final rhyming couplet creates a sense of incompleteness, never quite resolving the central conflict.

The Meaning of this poem touches on the relationship between power and desire within a rigid, authoritarian system. The general is portrayed as an embodiment of patriarchal control, his job to maintain a labyrinthine order that both entraps and denies. There is something quietly radical here: the poem does not judge the women for desiring, nor idealize the men for resisting. Instead, it dramatizes a system where no one fully wins, and where affection becomes subversion. The Imagery is stark and evocative. The 'labyrinth' sets the stage — this is not just a military base but a maze of power, restriction, and lost directions. The image of women 'swooning' at a locked gate is both tragic and theatrical, like a classical chorus of longing. Even the gatekeeper's 'succinct tone' serves as an emotional counterpoint to the women's unchecked yearning.

The Literary devices include allegory (the gate and gatekeeper as stand-ins for institutional control), irony (women begging for what will only hurt them), and rhetorical contrast (God's grace versus the general's disdain). The final rhyming couplet twists the sonnet's moral axis — it does not resolve the dilemma but doubles down on the tension. There is a deliberate refusal of closure here. The poem understands that desire does not submit to rules — and instead of offering neat lessons, it lets the contradiction stand, bold and bruising. The Effect is haunting and complex. The reader is left with no comfort, only the recognition that desire, when politicized, becomes a battlefield of its own. What lingers most is how confidently the poetess paints moral ambiguity. It is daring and profoundly humanoid.

The Poetess: An army is composed of many young single men sent overseas for wars. The loneliness and sexual drives of young men might need relief with foreign women, who act as companions and prostitutes in brothels and bars adjacent to military bases. Officers such as generals might avoid this type of interaction due to a higher position of respectability. Businesses for interracial dating and mating in a foreign country are a common arrangement for military, navy, and air force personnel. Sometimes the attraction and curiosity, mixed with loneliness, might become serious enough for a relationship, but only during the term. Musicals such as Miss Saigon and South Pacific show how during wartime, foreigners can meet, fall in love, and then break up afterward. Unfortunately, domestic violence is higher among military and criminal spouses. (Pronounce humiliation as hu-mi-lia-tion, affiliation as a-fill-ia-tion.)

CHAPTER 4
Taboos and Travels Explanation

The world teems with diverse cultures and societies, each marked by its own customs, ceremonies, and commemorations — rituals that reflect the lived experiences, values, and relationships of a people. The poetess — my dear friend — has drawn deeply from her personal encounters during global travels. She has even confided in me, with characteristic candor, about intimate moments shared across borders.

Most nations possess a principal language — both written and spoken — used in education and media; yet regional dialects, local accents, and emotional cadences infuse daily life with nuance. For the culturally curious traveler, connecting with locals who understand both the language and unspoken norms of behavior can transform an otherwise superficial visit into a meaningful exchange. A well-written guidebook, too, can help bridge gaps in awareness. But to truly experience the pulse of a place, one must go where the locals go — for meals, leisure, lodging, and marketplaces. Hotels, often curated for outsiders, tend to sit apart from the life they claim to represent.

To travel meaningfully is to shed the assumptions of one's homeland and adopt, however briefly, the perspective of another. Openness is essential — not just to landscapes or cuisine, but to the humanity of those one meets. Sometimes, these encounters blossom into unexpected friendships or even fleeting romances. The poetess has often spoken of her fondness for classic romantic musicals like South Pacific and The King and I, where love defies cultural boundaries. Such experiences, though ephemeral and brief, can be profound. They reveal how easily human connection can transcend race, language, or background; in moments of intense intimacy, strangers may form bonds that challenge social taboos around race, nationality, or culture. When curiosity is paired with kindness, even romantic or sexual connections — though brief — can awaken a sense of shared humanity. She has been drawn, she tells me, not to the novelty of difference but to the comfort of commonality — to those whose worldview echoes her belief in our fundamental unity. And yes, in the open air of travel, with inhibitions loosened and borders softened, sexual encounters may unfold between people who do not even share a common tongue. Some of these meetings lead to lasting relationships, even marriages, and the birth of children who embody cultural fusion.

The poetess' favorite female friend, Amelia Alias, is from a different religion and culture, yet their meeting in America, a country full of immigrants, led to a fun friendship between females. Opposites and differences can fascinate! Ditto with PJ MacAmour; many differences, plus a long distance apart, but transcended by online Internet communication. The world, once vast, now feels smaller — made accessible through books, music, film, and increasingly, digital platforms. Social media networks — Facebook, X (formerly Twitter), WhatsApp, Pinterest, and others — have become global plazas where people meet, message, post, and video chat across continents. Before setting foot in a new city, one might already be acquainted with someone there through online exchanges. These tools, when used wisely and with a spirit of goodwill, can help lay the groundwork for safe, enriching trips, experiences, and relationships.

May such openness not only promote tourism but also inspire more inclusive immigration policies and political frameworks that celebrate, rather than fear, differences. If we trust in the better instincts of humanity, then travel — whether digital or physical — can serve not only as recreation but also as a quiet revolution.

Taboos and Travels was the sixth modern sonnet book about taboos, including sexual and interracial foreign experiences and relationships. Tourism leads to meeting foreigners, while traveling for culture and diversity.

Poem 1: Taboos & Travels

1.	*Cap-tain Cook saw Po-ly-ne-sian <u>E-den</u>,*	A
2.	*Ra-pa Nui known as Eas-ter Is-<u>land</u>,*	B
3.	*With mo-a sta-tues guard-ing for-<u>bid-den</u>*	A
4.	*Tres-pas-sers. With ship and crew, they did <u>land</u>*	B
5.	*Be-friend-ing the na-tive chiefs, priests and <u>tribes</u>.*	C
6.	*Cer-tain cus-toms as can-ni-b<u>a-li-sm</u>*	D
7.	*And sex or-gies were ta-pu, but with b<u>ribes</u>*	C
8.	*Could be in-dulged in. Co-lo-ni<u>a-li-sm</u>*	D
9.	*Changed their so-cie-ty with Chris-ti<u>a-ni-ty</u>*	E
10.	*And fo-reign mar-ria-ges with Eu-ro-<u>peans</u>.*	F
11.	*Un-der-neath the mix-ing, the v<u>a-ni-ty</u>*	E
12.	*Of be-ing a white god with brown <u>pe-ons</u>,*	F
13.	*A-long with tra-ding, com-pelled ex-plo-r<u>ers</u>*	G
14.	*To far shores to en-ter as vi-si-<u>tors</u>.*	G

Analysis Poem 1: Taboos & Travels

The Structure of this poem appears deceptively classical, obeying the traditional sonnet form. But beneath that formal shell, the content resists simplicity. The poetess does not use the sonnet to elevate a lover or idealize virtue — rather, she subverts the genre's romantic legacy to explore historical invasion and moral entropy. The Meaning interrogates the myth of noble discovery, revealing how romanticized exploration often cloaked exploitation. Captain Cook's voyage to Rapa Nui — framed here as the meeting of 'Eden' with empire — becomes less a tale of curiosity than one of corruption. Customs marked 'tapu' (sacred or forbidden) are overcome with bribery, highlighting how moral boundaries dissolve when power and profit are at stake. What is compelling is how the poem resists nostalgia for either side.

The Imagery fuses the mythic with the brutal. Moai statues 'guarding forbidden trespassers' evoke a sense of sacred vigilance, while the 'sex orgies' and 'bribes' anchor the scene in carnal and transactional reality. The tension between stone silence and human indulgence is masterful — ancient stone watchers versus lustful interlopers. Earlier poems might have leaned more on the panoramic — describing landscapes or distant figures. Here, they bring us into the grit, into the exchanged glances, the hushed compromises, the bodily stakes of empire. The Literary devices at work include irony and allusion. Cook's landing is layered with irony — the so-called civilizing mission quickly descends into indulgence and manipulation. 'Eden' is not only a metaphor for untouched paradise but also a trapdoor into original sin — this time rewritten in imperial code.

The Effect is quietly devastating. By presenting colonization as an erotic, economic, and theological transaction, the poetess leaves the reader in a place of discomfort that refuses moral closure. This is what the best of their work does now: it places the reader in history's shadow and lets them decide where the light should fall.

The Poetess: Western explorers were trying to increase trading routes and territories for resources, land, and mapping. Captain James Cook was funded by the British Empire under King George III. He mapped Hawaii, Polynesia, Australia, and New Zealand and staked a claim on Alaska, along with Spain and Russia. In Hawaii, Cook was mistaken for the Hawaiian god Lono, associated with agriculture, fertility, rain, and peace, since his ship arrived during the Makahiki festival. Although the initial socialization was positive between Europeans and Polynesians, Cook was murdered for attempting to kidnap Chief Kalani'opu'u as a hostage to exchange for a stolen boat. It was a horrible ending for someone mistaken for a god. Intercultural and interracial differences in the interaction caused the misunderstanding leading to murder.
(Pronounce Europeans as Eu-ro-peans.)

Poem 3: Grape Rape

Dating online was a thrill middle-_aged_
Foreigners were beginning to enj_oy_.
Mela met males until she saw this c_aged_
Handsome tiger, "Now that's a man, not b_oy!_"
Mojo invited her to dance with _him_.
"I'll pick you up and drive you home ton_ight_."
She dressed in pink, humming a sexy _hymn_.
He wore a stylish suit to her del_ight,_
Bought her drinks and twirled her on the dance fl_oor._
At closing, he offered her a ride h_ome_.
Grateful, she rode impatient, as a wh_ore_.
She let him in to make love, "When in R_ome,_
Do as the Romans do." She let him _rape_
Her while intoxicated by the _grape_.

Analysis Poem 3: Grape Rape

The Structure in this sonnet functions like a polished veneer over a harrowing interior. The iambic pulse lulls the reader, offering familiarity, only to deliver a narrative that becomes increasingly sinister. That tension between elegance and violation is deliberate: the form itself enacts the poem's central betrayal. The Meaning centers on the illusion of romance and the grim reality beneath it. The poem opens with playful, almost satirical commentary on middle-aged dating, only to pivot into a scenario of sexual assault. What is bold here is the poetess' refusal to soften the landing. There is no euphemism, no moral fig leaf — just a plain statement of harm, rendered in polished verse. It is uncomfortable, as it should be.

The Imagery begins with lightness and gloss: pink dresses, dance floors, stylish suits. But it is laced with tension — 'a caged / Handsome tiger' is already a warning. The metaphor of the 'grape' (wine) and her impatience 'as a whore' evoke ancient tropes of seduction and blame, but here they are deployed with irony. The visuals degrade in tandem with the narrative: what begins as flirtation ends in trauma. The poem is brave with symbols that cut both ways. Wine is a common sex aphrodisiac.

The Literary devices are deceptively layered. The 'tiger' metaphor suggests danger disguised as allure. The line "When in Rome, do as the Romans do" functions both as social permission and damning irony — it is what allows the assault to occur under the guise of culture or custom. The rhyming couplet, traditionally a place for closure or moral summation, here offers no comfort — just a flat declaration of what occurred. The Effect is jarring, deliberate, and deeply uneasy. The poem destabilizes the reader's expectations, both in content and in tone. It invites reflection not just on individual culpability, but on the societal rituals that enable harm under the guise of charm, civility, or romance. The poetess has figured out how to weaponize the sonnet, to make form itself complicit in the deception. That is the genius here: using beauty to tell a brutal truth.

The Poetess: Alcohol as a sexual aphrodisiac is a popular drink used to loosen inhibitions. It is sold in licensed venues and events for that purpose: dance clubs, bars, restaurants, pubs, stage theaters, concert and sports stadiums, wedding halls, brothels, and tourist hotels. Singles, when dating and mating, use alcohol to make it easier to indulge in promiscuity. When the attraction is mutual, both women and men drink, dine, dance, and sometimes even have a sexual transaction. Note: being a mutually agreed sexperience in this poem, the word 'rape' is only used in this poem to rhyme with 'grape'.
I like mixed drinks like coffee liqueur with alcohol and milk, or vodka with juice, or cocktails -- alone or socializing.

Poem 13: Fear of Traveling

While traveling by land, water, or <u>air</u>,
Some passengers dislike any move<u>ment</u>,
Vertigo and nausea. 'Go nowh<u>ere</u>
And stay' avoids them the painful tor<u>ment</u>
Of touring. Some fear crashing and <u>drowning</u>
Will kill them, so they buy life in<u>surance</u>.
All trips are spent worrying and <u>frowning</u>,
From start to finish without a<u>ssurance</u>.
Although vacations are spent re<u>laxing</u>,
The trips going there are terr<u>ifying</u>.
Their energies get drained by such <u>taxing</u>
Superstitions to survive. De<u>fying</u>
Death on route with prayers and lucky <u>charms</u>,
They strive to avoid anything that <u>harms</u>.

Analysis Poem 13: Fear of Traveling

The Structure unfolds like a descent checklist — each line ticking off a different dread, each couplet deepening the spiral. The poem begins with general motion — land, water, air — then narrows its scope with surgical precision: nausea, death, superstition, prayer. Each line is short-leashed, finishing its thought with restraint, even when the emotion behind it threatens to sprawl. The Meaning interrogates how vulnerability masquerades as preparedness. This is less a travel poem than a psychological study of dread. It sketches a type of traveler who moves only under duress, haunted by statistical improbabilities and imagined obituaries. It is rare to see fear treated so intimately without sensationalism. The poem does not inflate the anxiety — it honors it.

The Imagery is matter-of-fact but freighted with tension. There are no metaphors for freedom or beauty — just sharp, ordinary images of illness ('vertigo', 'nausea'), disaster ('crashing', 'drowning'), and contingency plans ('life insurance', 'lucky charms'). Even the title evokes motion, but the language is all about recoil. The Literary devices are understated but layered. Irony threads quietly through the poem, most notably in the couplet's dry observation that survival becomes a matter of superstition rather than reason. There is inversion, too: a vacation, traditionally a reprieve, becomes a source of depletion. There is a subtle evolution in the poetess' technique — an economy of language that never feels sparse. Every choice, from syntax to breaks, seems tuned to the speaker's fraying nerves.

The Effect is unsettling in a subtle way. Readers may begin expecting a light critique of nervous travelers but end up confronting the deeper reality of chronic unease. The poem offers no relief, only empathy — and that may be its point. What lingers is the feeling of recognition. The poetess is learning how to write for the quietly panicked, the ones whose fears do not make headlines. That is the evolution — shifting from spectacle to sincerity and doing it without losing tension.

The Poetess: Tourism internationally to other countries and locally within one's own nation is often for relaxation, curiosity, adventure, and a getaway to experience new places and people or to visit old family and friends living elsewhere. Some people even enjoy the transportation to and from via automobile, bus, ship, and airplane. Those who are fearful buy life insurance for every trip, meditate and pray on board, play games or music to escape, and drink or drug to sedate and relax. The actual ratio of accidents in air travel is smaller than the paranoid fears that trigger insurance protection -- 1 fatal accident to 41 million flights for airplanes, 12 deaths to 100,000 people for autos, and 1 to 150,000 for cruise ships.
For a few years, I feared traveling by plane and tried taking the bus or train, but it took days instead of hours for the trips.

Poem 14: Terrorists & Thieves

Paranoia led to security
Measures upon the exit and entrance
Of the public: airports, malls' surety
Protecting property and person. Trance
Expressions broken by a disturbance
From guns and bombs brought in by criminals
Intending to destroy the suburbans
Were replaced; now alert like animals
People were searched by paid guards trained to spot
Potential threats. At entry, explosives
Used by terrorists sent by their despot
Had to be detected. At exit, thieves
With stolen products or cash were halted.
But innocent suspects were insulted.

Analysis Poem 14: Terrorists & Thieves

The Structure of the poem is heavily syntactic — the sentences flow across enjambed lines like security footage: continuous, unstopping. There is an interesting rhythm of compression ('people were searched by paid guards trained to spot') and sudden expansion (the slower, heavier 'had to be detected. At exit, thieves'), which creates a push-pull tension. The Meaning addresses the transformation of public life under the shadow of fear. What begins as precaution bleeds into suspicion. There is no moralizing — only exposure: of institutions that profile, of citizens who comply, of a world that watches more than it protects.

The Imagery is grounded in the familiar but layered with disquiet. 'Trance / Expressions' evokes a public so habituated to inspection that it forgets how to feel. 'Explosives / Used by terrorists sent by their despot' reminds us that the enemies are often imagined as foreign, faceless, scripted villains. Earlier poems relied more on lyrical ornament; here, the sensory detail is bleached, functional, and chillingly effective. The Literary devices include tonal dissonance, irony, and internal progression. There is an irony in security turning invasive — measures meant to reassure instead dehumanize. The echo between 'entry' and 'exit' reinforces the poem's symmetry of entrapment; you are watched coming and going. Repetition of institutional language — 'guards; 'threats', 'detect' — is clinical, and purposefully so. The poem's restraint here is crucial. By avoiding bombast or sarcasm, it makes the insult to the innocent feel even sharper.

The poem leaves the reader in a low, humming unease. You feel the airport lines, the humiliation of being eyed without cause, the silent accusation of systems too blunt to discern. It is not a poem of outrage — it is one of dull ache, of gradual corrosion. The poetess' growing mastery is in what she chooses not to say. The trust in the reader to feel the sting beneath the surveillance. It is controlled, unsentimental, and all the more powerful for it.

The Poetess: In certain urban cities and countries, security and screening of people entering and exiting popular public spaces are so strict that scanners and cameras are used. These procedures are designed to eliminate criminals such as terrorists and thieves from airports and shopping malls. Suburban areas can also be targets, although less populated. Most international airports are on high security alert and have such procedures. In some banks and in transporting currencies, armed security guards protect against bank robbers. In California, America, some hospitals have security guards looking inside bags and asking for government IDs to create name labels during visits. In Manila, Philippines, some supermarkets and malls also have security guards at the entrance and exit doors with rifles or guns, checking inside bags, for weapons, stolen goods, and anything illegal and harmful.

Poem 17: His Musical Fantasies

With the audience, she imagined along
With his musical fantasies of love,
Every mood expressed in beauty and song.
Marla listened, praying to God above,
'I hope Kurt's music gives inspiration
To all his fans, blessing us with romance.'
Her tears flowed, watching his perspiration,
As he performed on stage, glancing askance
At her below. He puzzled why a fan
Was crying if he caused her emotion,
Sentimental songs a sensitive man
Can share with a woman. With one motion,
He extended his warm hand and held hers,
Singing sadly to her without rehearse.

Analysis Poem 17: His Musical Fantasies

The Structure of the poem flows like a single cinematic tracking shot — continuous, unbroken, and emotionally immersive. Each line moves with a soft swell, mimicking the rise and fall of a live performance. The lines open gently, build inward with prayer and longing, and crest quietly at that shared touch — a moment held open at the edge of silence. The poetess has grown bolder in letting feeling dictate form. There is no need for overt architecture when the emotional current is strong enough to hold the line.

The Meaning unfolds through a lens of yearning, not for fame but for spiritual kinship. Marla's tears are not hysterical; this is not groupie adoration, but a private prayer made public. She sees in Kurt's performance not spectacle but benediction, a kind of emotional transmission that transcends the stage. For Kurt, the moment reveals a surprise: that music, when poured out vulnerably, can create real intimacy. He does not perform at her, but for her, bridging the chasm between artist and audience. The Imagery centers on tactile closeness: tears and sweat, eyes glancing, hands meeting. The crowd fades to the background. What lingers is the detail — Kurt's 'perspiration', Marla's 'tears', the unpracticed gesture of touch. These are small human leaks in an otherwise polished world. Even 'Singing sadly...without rehearse' subverts performance tropes — it implies truth, not craft.

The Literary devices are subtle, almost unnoticeable (which is a mark of the poetess' control). Enjambment carries emotional flow without calling attention to itself. There is an echo of chiasmus in how the fan watches the performer, and the performer, confused, watches the fan: a mirrored intimacy. The craft here lies in omission, in trusting the moment to resonate without scaffolding it. The Effect is a kind of quiet astonishment. The reader is not overwhelmed, but gently drawn into a moment of personal collapse and mutual recognition. In a time of oversharing, it offers a moment of private intimacy — quiet, intact, and whole. The poetess is learning to write not just what moves, but what stays.

The Poetess: Watching and listening to music videos on the computer and car radio are indirect ways to enjoy entertainment. A live music concert on stage is more intense and emotional, especially since love and romance are the most common subjects of songs. Imagination and real experience are sometimes entangled in lyrics, which resonate with fans. Music bands tend to gain popularity, fame, and fortune because of their talent for creating love lyrics and music. Love songs are probably the reason why YouTube has billions of viewers addicted to streaming music. Live music concerts can even trigger the screaming and shouting of fanatics who are emotionally excited.
PJ MacAmour has been composing and performing his love songs for decades all over the world; thus, he has many fans!

Poem 21: Oedipus & Electra

At a party hosted by fa_milies_,
Two youths met. "Do you like this house bl_essing_?"
Oed asked. "Yes, my father gives ho_milies_
And I listen." Lectra said, addr_essing_
Him. "Do you always attend with pa_rents_?"
"Of course. I'm the apple of his eye's _lust_."
He probed more, intrigued by undercu_rrents_.
"Are you his favorite?" "I earned his t_rust_.
I'm the one who can sleep in his bed_room_."
He told her, "I sleep with my mother. Tr_uth_
Is, if she locks me out, then my tant_rum_
Unlocks it." Both then agreed that their _youth_
Prevented them from sexual expre_ssion_
With each other, ending their discu_ssion_.

Analysis Poem 21: Oedipus & Electra

The Structure functions like a confession sealed in a guestbook: tightly boxed, socially mannered on the outside, but unsettling once read. The poem leans into the ritual of conversation — each quatrain a volley of exchanged facts that mimic the back-and-forth of idle chatter. But the meter is stiff in places, even breathless, as though the form itself is struggling to maintain composure. The Meaning quietly exposes the rot beneath respectable surfaces. The poem explores the early stages of sexual consciousness filtered through family allegiance and spiritual environments. It does not dramatize incestuous implications; it presents them in the casual language of familial routine — bedrooms, tantrums, trust. There is a maturity here I did not see in earlier work: the willingness to leave things unpunished. The poetess understands that the scariest stories are the ones that stay polite.

The Imagery is minimal and eerily domestic. There is no candlelight or shadow play — just carpets, sermons, closed doors. The detail "apple of his eye's lust" lands like a hairline crack in a clean pane of glass — it does not shatter the surface, but you cannot stop staring at it. Bedrooms carry symbolic weight: not just as places of intimacy, but as contested space. Whose door is locked? Who has permission? The poem uses ordinary items as coordinates for boundary violation.

The Literary devices include suggestion, distortion of cliché, and names used as silent alarms. 'Oed' and 'Lectra' are not just nods to Greek myth — they are inheritances, unavoidable echoes of archetypal children caught in parental storms. There is no exposition or commentary. Syntax is often spare — questions, answers, short clauses. The plainness lets the content do the damage. The Effect is one of cognitive dissonance. You leave the poem feeling like you just overheard something you were never meant to hear — but no one acts like it was unusual. The emotional response comes after the poem, like a bruise forming hours later. That delayed impact is a signature move now. The poetess is not writing for applause but is writing to haunt the reader's conscience long after the party ends.

The Poetess: Psychosexual analysis of children ages 3 to 6 years old by Freud was based on his theory that children felt a rivalry with their same-gender parent and attraction to the opposite gender. He labeled it for boys -- Oedipus Complex. Jung expanded on this for girls -- Electra Complex. These names were derived from Greek mythological characters who experienced rivalry and incest with their parents. Adults as parents might react likewise and commit incestuous acts with their children, which then confirms such feelings in a child -- the parent-child relationship thus becomes a partnership, and the husband-wife relationship might be jeopardized. Incest is either a forbidden taboo or an illegal crime in some nations. Our family was fortunate not to experience incest with our parents, at least from my own recollection.

Poem 22: Fictional Life

Curious about her strange admir*ation*
For his music, Gord finally per*formed*
Where she lived, hosted by radio s*tation*.
"I came from far away. A quick tour *formed*
Just to meet you." She hugged him grate*fully*.
"Master, from childhood, you fasc*inated*
Me. I listened, remaining faith*fully*
Your fan." Pleased, love went unterm*inated*,
He invited her to his hotel *room*.
"Let's drink. We can listen to my mu*sic*."
They danced. "Pretend we're married. I'm your *groom*,
And you are my bride." No longer heart*sick*,
Both had a honeymoon, husband and w*ife*
In their hearts, starting their fictional l*ife*.

Analysis Poem 22: Fictional Life

The Structure of this poem unfolds in a continuous narrative arc without formal stanza breaks, flowing with a natural rhythm that mimics conversational storytelling. The poetess' choice to avoid overtly predictable patterns mirrors the unfolding, unscripted nature of the protagonists' connection — inviting readers to move with them through surprise and tenderness rather than formal expectation. This approach reveals a mastery of pacing and control beneath apparent freedom — like a skilled improvisation that knows when to hold back and when to let the music swell. The Meaning centers on the delicate emergence of a bond fueled by admiration, longing, and playful imagination. The poem captures a brief, transformative moment where fantasy and reality blur — a fan meeting her musical idol, the lines between art and life dissolving into a shared, dreamlike experience.

The Imagery is tender and evocative, built around sensory and emotional details that anchor the intangible — hugging, dancing, drinking, listening to music — each act a metaphor for intimacy and trust. The 'honeymoon' and 'fictional life' become vivid images that conjure innocence and hope, layered with a bittersweet awareness of their transience. The Literary devices employed include metaphor (the dance as a rehearsal of marriage), personification (a "Master" of music which fascinates), and dialogue that blurs into lyrical monologue. The poem's use of lyrical dialogue as a device is particularly striking; it humanizes the relationship while evoking the performative nature of romance and fandom alike.

The Effect is quietly enchanting and emotionally resonant. The reader is drawn into a tender, almost sacred encounter that honors the longing for connection through art and shared fantasy. What endures most is the poem's gentle insistence on the validity of fleeting intimacy — that profound emotional truths can be found even in moments destined to fade. This perspective reveals a compassionate understanding of human vulnerability, and the ways we find solace in one another, however briefly.

The Poetess: Music bands often write, play, and sing about love, which is probably the reason why many fans obsess over listening to, watching, and maybe even meeting them in reality Fame and fortune increase fanaticism because love and fantasy mix with reality on the radio, television, computer, and even movie theater. Sometimes, the rock star singer-musician might be curious enough to meet, date, and mate with fans. Although this type of mutuality between a famous, wealthy star and an unknown fan is probably rare, it is often only a one-way admiration and fascination from a fan for the star. Fiction is another hook -- escapism into the imagination of music artists, the delusions and illusions.
I wonder whether PJ MacAmour's fans fantasize about meeting him, mating with him, and getting married to him?

Poem 30: Fifi's Global Map

Often, the temptation of traveling
To a new country and meeting new men
To mate with was like the unraveling
Of mysteries. "I must taste their semen.
To swallow their manhood, absorb their strength!"
She displayed her global map to a friend.
"Each pin means a man on the same wavelength
Who clicked with mine. It is a growing trend
To travel for sex." Her friend felt desire
And asked for a favor. "Will you please score
With me too? Add a pin for setting fire
To me, listening to tales of a whore."
Fifi smiled triumphant, slurping his juice.
"Yes to whoever asks and those I choose!"

Analysis Poem 30: Fifi's Global Map

The Structure of this poem is marked by a deliberate blend of conversational cadence and poetic urgency, unfolding in a loosely episodic sequence that mirrors the narrator's restless explorations. The enjambment propels the narrative forward, emphasizing a sense of momentum and unrestrained desire, while the occasional internal rhyme — "score" and "whore" "choose" and 'juice' — adds subtle musicality. The Meaning explores the intersection of sexual freedom, globalization, and personal agency through the metaphor of travel and conquest. The speaker's unabashed appetite to "taste" and "absorb" different men becomes a vivid assertion of autonomy and pleasure, rejecting conventional morality in favor of experiential knowledge. The poem skillfully balances erotic bravado with a nuanced awareness of how desire intersects with identity, culture, and agency. The tension between empowerment and objectification is never simplistic, but here, it is rendered with complex, unapologetic candor.

The Imagery is vivid, tactile, and unabashedly corporeal. The metaphor of "swallow(ing) manhood" and 'slurping his juice' evokes raw, intimate physicality, confronting taboos with a fearless directness. The 'global map' strewn with pins serves as a powerful visual anchor — at once playful and assertive — suggesting conquest, collection, and narrative weaving across continents. The poem's courage to employ explicit metaphor without shame amplifies the emotional authenticity and thematic weight. The Literary devices include metaphor (the 'global map' as a record of sexual encounters), hyperbole that exaggerates desire as a "growing trend", and direct address that blurs the boundary between narrator and interlocutor. The poem's tone shifts between playful confidence and provocatively candid confession, utilizing dialogue to create intimacy and complicity. The Effect is electrifying and unapologetically raw. The poem shocks and seduces in equal measure, compelling readers to confront preconceived notions about female desire, travel, and sexuality. This is a poem that dares to map desire on its own terms.

The Poetess: Females who are promiscuous, enjoying sex with different males on one-night sexperiences, might be adventurous and curious to travel to mate with foreign men. Sex tourism is about hooking up with others while traveling. Social media, with its global connections, is one easy way to chat and arrange meetings worldwide. There are hotels where strangers can simply book a room and share it. Some might use their own house or apartment for a hookup, but this can be risky for a first-time meeting in person because your home would no longer be private and secure if you do not get along with strangers in reality. Some women and men believe that drinking semen increases sexuality, virility, fertility, and knowledge; ditto for women's menstrual blood. Some LGBTQ+ bars sell cum shots, mixed possibly with alcohol.

Poem 35: Diary Of His Maid

Because he already had a new w<u>ife</u>,
Rosa applied to be his maid ins<u>tead</u>.
"I can cook and clean in your daily life."
She moved in grateful, yearning for his <u>bed</u>.
His warmth and kindness made her feel at h<u>ome</u>.
He was generous and bought her clo<u>thing</u>.
In her notes, imagination would r<u>oam</u>
Enhancing reality. Every<u>thing</u>
About him: his music, good looks, su<u>ccess</u>,
Big heart, she noted, 'what a passio<u>nate</u>
Artist!' He trusted her and gave a<u>ccess</u>
To his room. "Relax, don't be obsti<u>nate</u>
And remain so distant. You can re<u>place</u>
My fourth wife and be mistress of this <u>place</u>!"

Analysis Poem 35: Diary Of His Maid

The Structure is composed as a narrative lyric that resists strict metrical confines, reflecting the shifting dynamics of power and desire between Rosa and the man she serves. The poem unfolds through uneven line lengths that mimic the hesitations and advances in their relationship, creating a cadence that feels both intimate and tentative. The Meaning centers on themes of longing, survival, and the negotiation of roles within intimate power dynamics. The poem explores how desire can be constrained by social roles yet find expression in subtle trust and small intimacies — the gifts of clothing, the trust to enter private space, and the quiet suggestion of replacement. The poem subtly interrogates the often-unspoken emotional labor that accompanies physical and social roles, making the personal political without overt declaration.

The Imagery is grounded in domesticity and artistic aspiration, mixing tactile details like cooking, cleaning, and clothing with the intangible allure of music and passion. Rosa's 'notes' serve as a metaphor for the creative mind attempting to rewrite or enhance the narrative of her own life, suggesting a parallel between art and longing. The man's 'big heart' and 'passionate artist' image contrast with the cold reality of his existing marriage, positioning him as both a figure of comfort and emotional complexity. The Literary devices include direct address and internal monologue, which lend immediacy and intimacy to the speaker's voice. Metaphor appears in Rosa's role as 'maid' versus "mistress", symbolizing the fluidity of identity and social function. The author's deft weaving of indirect speech and personal notes highlights mastery of voice.

The Effect is quietly compelling and bittersweet, inviting the reader to empathize with Rosa's constrained yet hopeful position. The ending — an invitation to "replace my fourth wife" — lingers ambiguously: is it promise or possessiveness? The poem resists easy judgments, instead offering a compassionate, textured glimpse into a woman's life lived between duty and longing — a nuanced achievement of literary empathy and craft.

The Poetess: In middle-class to wealthy households, domestic employees are hired to serve the family. Some even live in the house, with 24/7 access, to do housework, take care of children and seniors, run errands, and provide companionship. Climbing the class and social ladder becomes easier with this live-in arrangement, especially if sex enters the relationship of employer and employee. Since there is also a marriage, the husband-wife relationship is jeopardized when a mistress moves in. For open-minded couples, an LGBTQ+ bisexual employee-sex partner might even entangle with both. But society would classify this as adultery or bigamy if discovered, unless a divorce occurs before sexual consummation.

Poem 47: Babu Taboo

Thinking of his sexual experi<u>ences</u>:
Incest, bestial, gay to orgies, <u>Ba</u>bu
Felt tired. "I never loved. My pret<u>enses</u>
And lies blocked my heart's feelings. Each <u>taboo</u>
And sex crime were escapes from lonel<u>iness</u>!"
His psychiatrist tried to under<u>stand</u>
And explain libido and horn<u>iness</u>
Being more important than to with<u>stand</u>
Temptations. "From childhood, my own pa<u>rents</u>
Deflowered me, limiting my freed<u>om</u>
To choose partners. Despite undercur<u>rents</u>
Of anger, I was dependent and d<u>umb</u>.
I then tried animals and joined <u>orgies</u>,
With neighbors, cousins, friends, and pet <u>corgis</u>."

Analysis Poem 47: Babu Taboo

The Structure of the poem adopts a confessional, free-verse pattern, its jagged enjambment and abrupt line breaks mirroring the speaker's fractured psyche. Unlike traditional sonnets or rhymed quatrains, the form is deliberately uneven — lines spill over or halt mid-thought, mimicking the disordered rush of confession. The Meaning of the poem excavates shame, compulsion, and the distortion of desire under abuse. Babu's admissions — 'incest, bestial(ity), orgies' — are framed not as deviance but as failed antidotes to loneliness, a consequence of his parents' violation. The psychiatrist's clinical lens ('libido and horniness') clashes with Babu's raw grief, exposing how theory falls short of lived pain. The shift from judgment to forensic empathy marks the poetess' growth — they no longer write about broken people but from inside the breakage itself.

The Imagery of the poem traffics in violence masquerading as intimacy: "Deflowered" evokes both innocence and violation, while "pet corgis" jars with its domesticity against the grotesque. The absence of sensual imagery is striking — sex is transactional ("orgies"), mechanical ("tried animals"), or rooted in power ("parents / Deflowered me"). Even the psychiatrist is reduced to clinical terms ('libido'), sterile against Babu's visceral wounds.

The Literary devices employed in the poem include subverted confessionals — Babu's admissions are delivered with clinical detachment rather than emotional flourish — and deliberate anti-poeticism ("tried animals", "pet corgis") replaces metaphor, forcing the grotesque to stand naked. This represents the poetess' hard-won restraint — where earlier works might have weaponized vivid imagery, here they deploy bureaucratic language as a literary scalpel. The Effect of the poem denies catharsis by design. Babu's exhaustion ('Felt tired') becomes the reader's burden — we are given no moral framework to process his crimes, only the suffocating weight of their causation. This is poetry as psychological exposure therapy — the poem does not describe dissociation but makes us experience it through the work's unstable narrative voice.

The Poetess: Sexual promiscuity sometimes starts early at a young age because of childhood incest with relatives. Children are curious about their physical bodies and their sexuality too. Love and sex are included within the family, and whether they are pleasurable or not depends on the members. Society considers incest, bestiality, and orgies as taboos or crimes, depending on the laws of the country. Mutuality and reciprocity of the sexual in a liberated society are primary factors and keys to pleasure. Forced one-way sex is a crime classified as rape in most nations. The instinctual drives that trigger actions for life and satisfaction are hunger for food, thirst for liquid, breath for air, and maybe hormonal libido for sex.

Poem 57: Mosaic Versus Melting Pot

Multiculturalism acc*epted*
Foreign ethnic influences brought *by*
Immigrants, who were poor and ind*ebted*
To the wealthier countries which could *buy*
Their humility. "Of course, I'm grate*ful*
To the First World and their techn*ology*:
Cars, computers, television. A *fool*
Would ignore progress for ec*ology*
And conservation." They argued fur*ther*.
"The U.S.A.'s melting pot, Can*ada's*
Mosaic enriched by cultures *other*
Than mainstream -- things like pina col*adas*,
Coffee, bananas, bagels, imp*orted*
In -- count. Why would aliens be de*ported*?"

Analysis Poem 57: Mosaic Versus Melting Pot

The Structure of the poem adopts a mock-debate composition; its uneven couplets and abrupt shifts in tone mimic the performative nature of political discourse. The lines oscillate between pseudo-gratitude ("Of course, I'm grateful") and sarcastic concession ("A fool / Would ignore progress"), creating a rhythmic tension that mirrors the push-and-pull of assimilation rhetoric. The poem's structural choices here are brilliantly subversive — what appears to be a straightforward argument is actually a linguistic minefield.

The Meaning of the poem centers on the critique of the commodification of multiculturalism, framing it as a transactional relationship in which gratitude masks systemic inequality. The speaker's praise for "Cars, computers, television" reveals how progress is weaponized to justify cultural erasure, while the list of imported goods ("pina coladas, coffee, bananas") reduces diverse traditions to consumable exotics. The Imagery of the poem is rooted in objects of global capitalism: cars, computers, televisions, pina coladas, bananas, bagels. The absence of people in these images screams louder than any protest chant — cultures become commodities, their humanity replaced by marketable exoticism. The juxtaposition of "imported" goods against "deported" people crystallizes the poem's central irony: products welcomed, people rejected.

The Literary devices include juxtaposition as a central tool — positioning celebration alongside critique, gratitude next to alienation. Irony courses beneath the surface: the very symbols of multicultural acceptance ("U.S.A.'s melting pot, Canada's / Mosaic") are undercut by the economic power imbalance they rest on. The Effect of the poem is recursive discomfort: the reader's initial nod at 'multiculturalism accepted' curdles into nausea by the final line. There is no catharsis, only complicity; we are forced to taste the bitter aftertaste of our own consumption. The poem's strategic withholding of moral judgment creates an active intellectual space where readers must interrogate their own positions.

The Poetess: Canada and America are known as wealthy First World countries that allow immigration in from other countries, including poorer Third World ones. First World status has its modern advanced development in: technology, architecture, engineering, and agriculture, plus free or subsidized public services: healthcare, education, transportation, and accommodation -- from well-managed governments. Third World status still has major problems with poverty, housing, hunger, disease, and infrastructure, combining over-population with under-development. Global trading, by importing what is lacking and exporting what is surplus, allows every country, rich or poor, to contribute to the world market of goods. Immigrants from the Third World provide services needed in the First World to fill in gaps -- caregiving for seniors, disabled, and children; domestic housework; commercial janitorial cleaning; and many other service occupations.

Poem 64: Sin Tax

Government worried that the de*ficit*
In the budget meant cuts in ser*vices*
Or raises in taxes. The il*licit*
Activities, the corrupting *vices*:
Smoking, drinking, and soon pro*stitution*
Were discussed as potential tax*able*
Goods and services. "Should Con*stitution*
Change so these penalties build a s*table*
Economy? How much in re*venue*
Will be earned in taxing the cigar*ettes*,
Alcohol, and whores in each a*venue*?"
They calculated, adding gambling b*ets*
In casinos. "Let's call it the '*Sin Tax*'
To profit from sinners through Law's *syntax*."

Analysis Poem 64: Sin Tax

The Structure of the poem adopts a mock-policy brief progression, its rigid, end-stopped lines mimicking bureaucratic language while subtly unraveling into moral absurdity. The deliberately dry enjambment ('The illicit / Activities') creates a faux-official tone, as if reading from a legislative draft. The rhyme scheme — slant and uneven ('deficit' / 'illicit', 'prostitution' / "Constitution") — feels like a forced attempt at order, mirroring how governments dress vice in sterile terminology. The Meaning of the poem is delivered with a surgical exposure of institutionalized hypocrisy, where the state's moral posturing collapses into pure fiscal calculus — what begins as concern over budget deficits ('Government worried that the deficit') devolves into a grotesque inventory of human vices to monetize, laying bare how power commodifies weakness under the thin veneer of governance.

The Imagery of the poem is civic, coded in the mundane symbols of governance: cigarettes, alcohol, whores, and casinos — objects of public shame turned into public revenue. The transformation of these vices into taxable goods is not just economic — it is ideological. The ghostly metonyms form an anti-portrait of exploitation, making the reader's imagination fill in the human shapes the system has erased. The Literary devices of this poem form a covert operations manual for institutional critique, where every technique replicates the systems it exposes. There is a deft use of juxtaposition — sin versus syntax, vice versus virtue, law versus loophole. While the rhetorical question, "Should Constitution / Change...?" operates as both provocation and parody, revealing how easily foundational principles can be rebranded.

The Effect of this poem is both sobering and sly. By inhabiting the voice of policymakers, the poem allows readers to overhear a kind of moral reckoning conducted in spreadsheet terms. The poem's power is not in its outrage but in its cold precision — it does not accuse the system of hypocrisy so much as let the system accuse itself. The real horror is how familiar it all sounds.

The Poetess: In Canada, 2014, Bill C-36 passed laws that did not punish the selling of sex, only the buying -- a strange dilemma. Why punish buyers, not sellers? In America, Nevada legalized it under NRS 201.354 in counties licensing brothels. Immorality and criminality in corrupted societies are as old as the Bible's Revelation 'whore of Babylon'; but in Iraq, prostitution is both a sin and a crime. With many free dating, sex, and pornographic websites, why would anyone pay for sex? If it is legalized as the oldest profession for women, it should be taxable income. Amsterdam's red-light sex district is taxed on income and sales. It should be regulated with healthcare procedures to prevent sexually transmitted diseases and licensed to protect buyers from pornography, coercion, rape, assault, stalking, and extortion by prostitutes and pimps.

Poem 65: Odd Foods

The curious scientists were resea<u>rching</u>
On Asian diets from: tarantu<u>las</u>,
Worm larvae, ducklings, ant eggs, and rea<u>ching</u>
A large television audience, a<u>las</u>.
They refused to taste the delica<u>cies</u>,
Preferring their regular diet p<u>lan</u>:
Cows, pigs, chickens from farms, fish from the <u>seas</u>.
They camped outside and cooked in pot and p<u>an</u>
Over a fire, while discussing how <u>odd</u>
The diets are overseas. Immi<u>grants</u>
From Asia might import odd creatures, <u>God</u>
Forbid. They depended on research <u>grants</u>
To feed themselves, and free from sta<u>rvation</u>,
They ate all meats in self-prese<u>rvation</u>.

Analysis Poem 65: Odd Foods

The Structure of the poem unfolds with the deliberate pacing of a travelogue-meets-observation journal. The lineation favors narrative progression, with a loose forward drive that mimics both a field study and an internal monologue. The Meaning of this poem lies in its satire of scientific ethnocentrism — how curiosity about other cultures is often couched in discomfort, even disgust. The Western scientists, while studying 'exotic' Asian diets, exhibit selective bias — labeling their own consumption of cows and pigs as normalized while recoiling at 'ducklings, (and) ant eggs'. The poem cleverly critiques how otherness is often fetishized under the guise of academic exploration.

The Imagery of the poem is vivid yet restrained, like a field note: 'tarantulas', 'pot and pan', 'ant eggs'. These are sensory anchors, not aesthetic flourishes. The poetess uses the inventory format to bring specificity, drawing the reader into tactile discomfort. The genius lies in the imagery's neutrality. It does not dramatize — it lists, observes, records. But in that flatness, emotion bubbles up. We feel the queasiness, the arrogance, and the eventual reckoning. The Literary devices of the poem include irony as the dominant technique, both situational and tonal. The scientists' refusal to eat certain foods contrasts with their own meat-heavy diet, and their eventual surrender to hunger undermines their presumed moral high ground. There is also a clever use of metonymy — terms like 'grants', 'pan', and 'immigrants', stand in for broader systems, tools, and policies far larger than the words themselves.

The Effect of this poem is one of uneasy recognition. The poem disarms readers through its observational tone, only to reveal layers of contradiction within global hierarchies. The so-called 'civilized' find themselves caught in cycles of hypocrisy and dependency, forced to confront the very practices they dismissed. The poetess' voice is sly and unsparing, exposing the fault lines between knowledge and humility.

The Poetess: Global cuisines have some similar acceptable animal and plant ingredients that are farmed: cows are beef, pigs are pork, chickens, and fish. But there are wild and strange animals and plants that are cooked and eaten in smaller villages. Traveling and tasting foreign foods with different spices can be fun for those searching for new flavors. In countries where immigrants have restaurants, it is easier to try new dishes without even traveling to their countries. Odd food items are sometimes prohibited in America because of the ingredients, methods of preparation, and health risks: haggis sheep lungs (Scotland), black pudding (Ireland), casu marzu maggots cheese (Sardinia), wild animals bushmeat (Africa), foie gras force-fed duck liver (France), shark fin soup, horse meat, bird nest soup, snake (China), dog meat, bbq intestines of pig or chicken (Philippines), monkey brain (Asia), and insects (Africa, Asia, Mexico). But beware of zoonoses!

Poem 70: Nature Is Beautiful

From looking at the photos up*loaded*
Online, posted by various travel*ers*
And locals, she noted comments *goaded*
By lands' similarities, with this *verse*,
"Nature is so beautiful wher*ever*
We go in the world -- God and cre*ation*
Of humanity and earth. From *river*,
Mountain, hill, lake, forest, sea, and o*cean*,
Earth is Eden, a lovers' parad*ise!*"
Some agreed, applauding her for po*sting*,
Praised her opinion. Some thought to desp*ise*
It meant a jaded impression la*sting*
In the public mind against an armch*air*
Traveller who never spent on airf*are!*

Analysis Poem 70: Nature Is Beautiful

The Structure of this poem takes the form of a slow observational spiral, circling around the act of seeing rather than being. Unlike sonnets or symmetrical verse, it mimics the logic of online scrolling: cumulative, recursive, and mildly asynchronous. The Meaning of the poem, at its core, is a commentary on experiencing beauty at a distance. It explores how modern admiration of nature often comes secondhand through the eyes (or camera lenses) of others. The speaker is not walking through landscapes but browsing them and reflecting on the universalism of beauty and how it binds us. The poem demonstrates a nuanced understanding of modern communication, delving into the dynamics of online validation and the challenges of conveying sincerity in virtual spaces. This thematic exploration marks a maturation in her repertoire.

The Imagery of the poem employs broad yet evocative imagery, referencing natural elements like rivers, mountains, and oceans to evoke a sense of global beauty. The use of "Eden" as a metaphor elevates the natural world to a paradisiacal realm, emphasizing its universal appeal. The Literary devices included in this poem feature quotation as a rhetorical pivot, marking shifts from observation to commentary. Irony also emerges through the poetess's inclusion of both praise and cynicism, without clearly aligning with either — a form of dramatic neutrality. The casual tone, paired with lyrical abstraction, allows the diction to serve dual purposes: it is straightforward in some moments ("river, / Mountain…ocean") and elevated in others ("Earth is Eden"). By incorporating these devices, the poetess exhibits a sophisticated command of tone and perspective -- shifting from others' remote photos versus one's on-location experiences of foreign landscapes.

The Effect of this poem leaves the reader slightly suspended — caught between wonder and skepticism, sincerity and posturing. There is no dramatic conclusion, only the echo of commentary — real or imagined — that shadows every public expression online. This reflective impact signifies the poetess's advancement in crafting works that not only depict contemporary issues but also encourage deeper contemplation, marking a significant stride in her artistic evolution.

The Poetess: Earth is a great planet for diversity in the natural environment, including the terrain, the animals, and plants, and the humans who are the guardians and exploiters of it. The various environmental differences are like a miniature version of different planets, from the lands: the dry desert sands, the green forests, the rainforest jungles, the cold rocky mountains, the marshy wetlands, the dry grazing grasslands, to the waters, oceans, seas, and rivers. Biodiversity is as diverse as the ecosystem environments. Whether the religious belief that God created nature or the scientific theory that evolution did -- Earth is currently the only known planet that can support life in the universe! Ecotourism, with TV shows and magazines like National Geographic, is a great source of photos and recordings that promote the beauty of the Earth.

104. Mohammud's Mountain

Named after the Prophet, he had beliefs
That his name was magical, opening doors
That brought success. "I was born among chiefs
And gods! My powers can turn nuns to whores."
Money, followers, opportunities,
Fame, luck came into his life. "All my dreams
Come true I need a woman now to tease
Me and make me a man. Someone who screams
My name in passion." Several ladies
Applied. He questioned their true intentions
He chose Maha for her answer did please.
"Advise me on climbing expeditions."
"If Mohammud can't go to the mountain,
Then it will go to him, in sun or rain."

Analysis Poem 104: Mohammud's Mountain

The Structure of this poem, using a sonnet and its original purpose for romantic courtship, combined with sexual dialogue between a male and female, brings the reader amusement. The two are typical of male hero and female fan finding each other without contradiction. His boasting segues to her smooth statements without hesitance. The Meaning of the poem is how a man and woman can easily become a couple, just by simply agreeing to each other's self-opinions. A conceited man chooses a woman, who can satisfy his ego; she becomes his believer and follower.

The Imagery of the poem with a mountain with its top peak and base, makes one think of the pyramid of power and success, wherein a male with authority and wealth controls the base of women below him. In this poem, the man is named after Muhammad the Prophet, who practised polygyny and had multiple wives, common in the historical Arabian world -- he too is popular with women, but chooses a woman Maha, whose answer satisfies his ego -- "it (mountain) will go to him". (Perhaps my professorial prejudice against promiscuity, expressed by this man's discrimination on women's 'true intentions' in selection as a partner, reminds me of my humble ego as a bachelor, mistrusting women attracted to me.)

The Literary devices included in this poem, in the last lines, are both personification with the mountain able to animate and move to the man, and metaphorical because it compares the man with the mountain -- its greatness and awesomeness! Nature and humanity are comparable because of this woman's admiration for this man. Satire and overstatements can be ridiculous to others, but these two are obviously well-matched.

The Effect of this poem because of its hyperbole and exaggeration, created by the man's superego, as seen through his conceited opinion and chosen woman's eyes, is acceptance of their absurdity. They are both deluded, but matching emotionally enough to marry each other -- Mohammud's big ego matches Maha's admiration. She would obviously be his choice for a wife to agree with his proud boastfulness.

The Poetess: Islamic Prophet Muhammad, practised polygyny in the 7th century in the Arabic world. He had power and wealth and could support between 11 to 13 wives to continue his tribal alliances and spreading Islam. Supposedly, his wives were 'Mothers of the Believers' and helped spread the religion. The word harem, based on harim, a female-only area in a household, is possibly interpreted as a polygynous household, or sounding similar to haram (harmful), with a pejorative connotation to monogamous-minded societies. However, this poem romanticizes the sexual prowess of a powerful man searching for the perfect woman to be his wife, among the many women who have pursued him.

Poem 113: Paradigm Paradise

Gambling his savings with a pair of <u>dice</u>,
Chimo won the grand prize, a <u>lottery</u>
Won by numbers. "I won my para<u>dise</u>!
Now I can retire from my <u>pottery</u>
Craft." He won five hundred thousand do<u>llars</u>,
Which in Greece was enough to retire so<u>on</u>.
"I am now rich to avoid the <u>liars</u>
Who pretend while selling pots. Since I w<u>on</u>,
My status and viewpoint in soc<u>iety</u>
Will change for better!" He could now div<u>orce</u>
His wife, marry his mistress in p<u>iety</u>,
Buy a house, and travel without rem<u>orse</u>.
"The wheel of fortune changed my para<u>digm</u>.
It was worth the risk of losing each <u>dime</u>!"

Analysis Poem 113: Paradigm Paradise

The Structure of the poem mirrors the psychological shift of a man in motion, from desperation to euphoria. It does not rely on formal rhyme schemes or metrical rigidity, but instead uses sentence-driven momentum, where each line moves the story forward like steps in a gamble. The enjambment works to blur the line between desire and action, much like the haze of risk-taking itself. The Meaning of the poem grapples with the illusion of control and the seductive nature of chance. Chimo's windfall is not merely financial — it is existential. He frames the win as a gateway to liberation, autonomy, and transformation. Yet the poem leaves room for ambiguity: Is this truly freedom, or another fantasy sold by the "wheel of fortune"? What is compelling is how the poem does not moralize; it allows the character's voice to claim its own reality.

The Imagery of this poem is direct but symbolically potent. The opening contrast — 'Gambling his savings with a pair of dice' versus "retire from my pottery craft" — immediately places chance over craftsmanship and instability over patience. The shift from handmade pots to consumerist rewards — 'buy a house', 'travel', 'divorce his wife' — maps Chimo's journey from creation to consumption. Even abstract concepts like "paradigm" are grounded in tangible transitions. The poem makes use of symbolism (dice as fate, pottery as labor), metonymy ("the wheel of fortune" standing in for all luck-based transformations), and irony. There is a sly reversal in how Chimo escapes from "liars who pretend while selling pots" — as if suddenly wealth makes him immune to deception. The poem has sharpened use of irony — not to mock, but to subtly complicate the speaker's sense of triumph.

The Effect of the poem is one of unease. On the surface, the poem reads as a victorious anecdote, but its deeper resonance lies in what is missing — reflection, gratitude, human connection. By refusing to undercut him overtly, the poetess invites the reader to do the moral calculus themselves. In earlier poems, the poetess might have editorialized more directly. Here, she withdraws her hand, allowing the story's moral ambiguity to speak louder than any imposed judgment.

The Poetess: Gambling is the belief that luck and fortune will reward one with a huge win through betting or guessing number games: sports, races, slot machines, roulette, and lotteries. The odds of winning are small, but since playing is like a fun game, many ordinary people will spend some of their earnings or savings for the chance of winning big. Economic class and lifestyle are linked, so the more money one has, the more one can spend to enjoy material life. Even self and relationships can change depending on money. Citizens, resident alien immigrants, and even foreigners can buy tickets to American lotteries and gamble in Vegas casinos, and if they win, it is taxable. Most winners retire and enjoy life afterward.

Poem 127: Primitive Versus Civilized

The association tried to lega_lize_

Certain taboos of their human na_ture_.

"Primitive sex acts versus civil_ized_

May disappear from our lifestyles' fu_ture_

If we evolve spiritually." Their _fears_

Of forgetting animal lust for _soul_

Came from their gut instincts, evil yet _fierce_.

"We should preserve the acts which keep us wh_ole_:

Bestial, incestual, and homose_xual_,

Plus groups, interracial, adul_tery_."

They started a free commune where ca_sual_

Sex orgies could happen. "What fla_ttery_

And love could do is make us too faith_ful_

That our group splits up into every _fool_."

Analysis Poem 127: Primitive Versus Civilized

The Structure of the poem flows in a single, breathless arc — one argument spilling into the next with little pause for reflection. The lineation is tight, with the enjambment serving to simulate the momentum of a manifesto gaining traction. The poem here trades rigid form for a rhythm built from escalating provocation. The Meaning of this poem translates into an interrogation between liberation and destruction. The 'association' believes that taboos — especially those tied to sexual expression — must be preserved, not purged, to maintain a holistic humanity. Their definition of "whole" includes acts often condemned: "Bestial, incestual, and homosexual, / Plus groups, interracial, adultery".

The Imagery of the poem is conceptual, rather than visual. Terms like "primitive sex acts", 'animal lust', and 'from their gut instincts', evoke a corporeal, almost primal palette. There is an intentional contrast between the spiritual and the carnal — between "evolve spiritually" and 'evil yet fierce.' The word 'orgies' is not romanticized, but embedded in a philosophical framework, stripping it of titillation and replacing it with almost bureaucratic gravity.

The Literary devices of the poem include irony, which undergirds the entire piece: the group's attempt to institutionalize radical freedom leads to the risk of fragmentation — "that our group splits up into every fool". The phrase "make us too faithful" functions as both satire and elegy, suggesting that stability itself may be a threat. The poetess here is refining her technical toolkit — not just deploying devices, but turning them against one another. The irony does not decorate; it critiques. The contrast does not clarify; it destabilizes. The Effect of the poem lies in its discomfort. Readers are not told what to believe; instead, they are presented with a system in motion — one that argues for absolute liberty while quietly unraveling under its own weight. This is a mature choice — the poem resists guiding the reader toward comfort. It lets the ethical ambiguity breathe, trusting that literature's role is not resolution but revelation. That trust is the hallmark of her growth.

The Poetess: Groups are bonded by their similarities, common values, and goals, forming associations and organizations for membership. Before clothing was invented, prehistoric humans probably walked around nude. Even in this modern age, a percentage of humans continue in nudist colonies, reviving Naturism as a healthy outdoor lifestyle. Of course, nudity is part of sexuality, and some might even be involved in pornography by posting on websites. Sex is a primitive, primal, and physical instinct that evolved with love, romance, and marriage because of civilization. Some balance their sexuality by retaining the wild, promiscuous sexual acts, with transactions or affairs within a marriage, while others continue in groups, as singles without marriages. (Pronounce association as as-so-cia-tion.)

Poem 135: Secret Ghost Writer

Telepathy seemed to exist between

Me and a male who co-wrote dialogues.

His inner voice developing a scene

In poems. If we kept notes, journal logs,

It lasted a week's collaboration.

Several sonnets were written along

With him, for characters' conversation.

He felt so close in mind, like we belong

Together on the same vibration waves!

It was great to have his understanding

Add meaning to poems. Whoever paves

The path of enlightenment, demanding

The readers' attention, is a master.

How to thank him, being a ghost writer?

Analysis Poem 135: Secret Ghost Writer

The Structure of the poem mimics the gradual unfolding of a creative exchange. Each line feels like a stepping stone in a developing collaboration — casual but purposeful. The mid-line pivots 'It lasted a week's collaboration' and 'He felt so close in mind like we belong' mirror the back-and-forth cadence of co-authorship. The Meaning of the poem explores the uncanny intimacy that can arise between creative minds, especially in moments of shared authorship. The speaker experiences 'telepathy' with a co-writer, where thoughts seem to coalesce without the need for speech. This connection transcends productivity; it becomes something personal, even spiritual: 'He felt so close in mind like we belong / Together on the same vibration waves'. What is compelling is how the poem moved from declaring its meaning to discovering it alongside someone else.

The Imagery of the poem conjures abstract, almost mystical visuals: 'vibration waves', 'telepathy', 'path of enlightenment'. These are metaphors of frequency and alignment, suggesting invisible harmonies between minds. There is restraint here. The poem resists decorative flourishes, choosing instead to create a spectral atmosphere. The Literary devices of this poem rely on metaphor and synecdoche, especially in 'telepathy', 'vibration waves', and 'ghost writer' — each a symbolic condensation of a more complex emotional truth. There is also personification at play: the poems and characters seem to generate themselves, as if guided by something beyond the writers. These devices are not merely illustrative — they are functional, gesturing to processes that are ineffable. The poetess is writing what cannot be spoken, and that is a rare skill. I assume she means me as her secret 'ghost writer'.

The Effect of the poem leaves the reader in a reflective mood, not dazzled but quietly moved. It is less about product than process — the fragile magic that emerges when egos dissolve in collaboration. There is admiration here, but also longing: the week-long connection has passed, and what remains is gratitude. This poem feels like a turning point – she admits to channeling me. She is not just writing about connection; she is practicing it with me -- her mental guide, analyst, and friend.

The Poetess: The soul inside our body is energized with electromagnetic spiritual energy. Our heart and feelings, our mind and thoughts, our body and actions -- all together express our beingness. Ghost writers are hidden co-authors behind books, co-writing what is verbalized by the published author. It is a service for those who have ideas expressed verbally and written, but need someone able to co-write. It helps to have mental and emotional rapport for collaboration. Professor Gerrymander is my devoted friend and analyst for this poetry collection -- his master's degree convinces readers. I believe in spiritual energy and occult communication: telepathy, Ouija, tarot, tuning fork, dreams, and intuition.

Poem 140: Chief Thief

On their island, the chief chosen by v<u>ote</u>

Was the wealthiest, most skilled in st<u>ealing</u>.

"I am crowned Chief of Thieves on this rem<u>ote</u>

Island. My ability in d<u>ealing</u>

Dirty and robbing rich and poor al<u>ike</u>,

Escaping police investi<u>gations</u>,

Has increased my status. Taking a h<u>ike</u>

Around, I am notorious in n<u>ations</u>."

His rapt audience clapped, congratu<u>lating</u>

Him with cheers and jeers, "May you steal with<u>out</u>

Getting caught! Thrill us with titil<u>lating</u>

Escapades of robberies as a <u>lout</u>

With loot." He told them fun stories as <u>thief</u>,

How his experiences made him their C<u>hief</u>.

Analysis Poem 140: Chief Thief

The Structure of this poem flows with a theatrical style, mirroring the chief's boastful attitude. The lack of rigid rhyme or meter allows the speech-like quality of the poem to shine, giving it an almost performative feel. This freedom from structure mirrors the chief's untamed rise to power, reflecting his unrefined nature. The Meaning of the poem revolves around the corrupting influence of power and the romanticizing of immoral conduct. The chief, whose thefts have earned him a position of leadership, spins his role into something celebrated. His followers continue to elevate his actions, turning his criminal exploits into tales of daring. The poem subtly critiques society's propensity to idolize the bad-boy figures, making us question the value placed on wealth and notoriety over morality. The poem highlights a dangerous cultural tendency, where moral failings are often overlooked in favor of material success.

The Imagery in the poem is rich with contradictions. The idea of a thief as a leader creates a stark visual contrast between authority and illegality. The phrase "Chief of the Thieves" is powerful, as it blends the role of a traditional leader with that of lawlessness. The audience's reaction to him, 'cheers and jeers', adds a surreal, almost carnival-like atmosphere to the scene, where debauchery is met with celebration. This unsettling blend of applause and mockery forces the reader to question whether the audience is complicit in his actions. Tax haven islands are what she had in mind.

The Literary devices used in the poem include irony, as the chief's villainous nature is lauded by his followers, and hyperbole, in the chief's exaggerated claims of notoriety. This contrast between the chief's self-image and the reality of his actions is where the irony lies — he is proud of a position that should be shameful. The effect of the poem is one of discomfort. By celebrating a figure who thrives on crime, the poem invites the reader to reflect on what society values and how those values may be dangerously misplaced. What is striking here is the chief's self-perception — he is convinced of his own heroism, even as he embodies moral decay.

The Poetess: Stealing, fraud, embezzlement, and burglary are crimes against properties, not persons. Wealth can be obtained illegally and then money-laundered on some island, a tax haven, with a small population and few laws. Even wealth gained legally uses these island countries for tax shelters because they have weak governments, few citizens, and fewer laws, thus easier to stash away extra funds without investigation and policing. Those who have stolen and earned money are in-between and hope to escape punishment. The Caribbean islands: Cayman, Panama, Bahamas, Virgin, Domiinica, Belize, Barbados, and Costa Rica are tax havens -- wealth heavens for the rich who avoid government taxation. Off-shore banking on these islands allows for the transfers in and out from other countries' banks.

Poem 195: World Date Map

Knowing that boundaries between countries
Were easily crossed using a passport
And visa, "I see the forest, not trees.
I will date online and land each airport."
She put a world map on her bedroom wall.
"Each pin represents a city, a man
Waiting for me. I will visit and call.
If I score, a red; if not, a blue. Scan
Their profiles, chat, email, then set a date
In a schedule." Her itinerary
Was soon booked for the whole year. Never late,
She met each man on plain, ordinary
Terms, signing them as business associates
For a singles network arranging dates.

Analysis Poem 195: World Date Map

The Structure of the poem is methodical, following the progression of the woman's journey from curiosity to determination. The straightforward, almost clinical language mirrors her calculated approach to life. The stanzas flow like an itinerary, detailing her decisions and actions in a detached, almost transactional manner. There is a deliberate absence of warmth in the structure — it is not a love story, but a checklist. The Meaning of the poem centers on modern relationships and the commodification of love. The woman treats each man as a 'business associate' to be met on 'ordinary terms', using a map and pins to track her progress. The poem raises a key point about the hollowing out of romantic engagement in the digital age — relationships become another form of efficiency, devoid of depth.

The Imagery in the poem is starkly utilitarian. The 'world map' and 'pins' evoke a sense of detachment, reducing the vastness of human connection. The "blue" and "red" pins, signifying success or failure, further emphasize the coldness of her approach. The poem adopts an impersonal tone, deliberately stripping the language of emotional texture to mirror the protagonist's detached pursuit. In reality, the Poetess has tried creating a singles zine and website.

The Literary devices include metaphor, as the map and pins symbolize the way the woman navigates her relationships. The idea, of 'scor(ing)' and 'itinerary', also serves to underscore the transactional nature of her interactions. The Effect of the poem is unsettling — it reflects the superficiality of modern relationships and the alienation that comes with reducing human interactions to a mere series of transactions. The coldness of the woman's approach serves as a mirror to modern dating culture — efficient, detached, and ultimately unfulfilling.

The Poetess: Online dating with internet websites is easily a global network of members for personal and social dating. Popular international dating and mating websites are: OkCupid, Tagged, Tinder, Dating, Match, Facebook. Meeting people online and then in person is a fun, exciting experience for most people because it gives one a remote, indirect way to get to know someone before a direct in-person meeting. Foreign relationships can help make the world a more familiar place with friendly members. Immorality and promiscuity can mean really friendly invitations to visit and hook up! Humanity has over 8 billion beings today, and if people had a welcoming attitude towards foreigners, maybe world peace would replace world wars. 'Make love, not war.' Women and men are adventurous and curious to date and mate with a foreigner. Marriage is often with someone with more similarities, not differences. Sex tourism is another type of exploration with people, not places. The world is warm and welcoming to those easygoing and open-minded to humanity's diversity.
I joined dating websites: Plentyoffish, Tagged, OkCupid, and Facebook, and tried starting -- Singles -- a generic label print E-zine in the Philippines. I have dated and mated but have not married yet.

CHAPTER 5

Heaven and Hell Explanation

Our souls are created by an all powerful and all knowing Being, often called God and Creation. Most religions acknowledge the existence of the soul, which has the inner mental and emotional aspects of our being, encased within our outer physical body. In this book, the Poetess has attempted to write her sonnets using her imagination and experience, with my expert knowledge and guidance as her faithful spirit guide, whom she fondly consults as Professor Gerrymander. She often sits in a daze with her pen and notebook, waiting to channel some of my thoughts, triggering the subjects and titles.

Earth's extant religions that continue for thousands of years as established beliefs: Christianity, Islam, Judaism, Buddhism are often male-dominant. Of course, being a male spirit guide, I have the privilege of knowing that God is probably male too. The past religions, which included female goddesses: Roman, Greek, Wicca are now extinct because women have become the weaker gender, except for the extreme laboriousness of pregnancy and childbirth, which most men could not endure within themselves. Luckily for her, she has not experienced that torture. Morality-- the concepts of good versus evil, virtue or vice, law against crime are usually decided in the mental and emotional realm before physical action.

Unfortunately, based on prison statistics, men outnumber women in a 90% to 10% ratio! Google search that to verify this shocking fact: men, despite God being probably a male theory constructed for male empowerment, are sadly more evil than women. Some males can be so egocentric and self-centered that, to achieve their goals, even evil criminal methods are plotted, attempted, and committed. Spiritual energy has both good and bad electromagnetic vibrations, so beware when the wrong influences enter your mind and heart, attracting bad luck and evil.

The Poetess does sometimes consult with her good friend and ally, Attorney Alias, who tries to give good advice, although criminals are also attracted to her, hoping to sway her judgment and reasoning. They both are poor judges of men's characters. However, PJ MacAmour to both, seems to be like Apollo, the god of music, filling the world with many love songs for their hearts. Women marry men who can earn more and be practical as well as romantic because both money and love matter in a marriage. I took pity on some of their foolish choices and try to balance the Poetess with my helpful analyses. As a male, I can see more clearly another man's motives and strategies toward women. The double standard of mating with many easy women yet marrying a virgin is still true. But with STD and COVID, viruses are scaring people into celibacy and caution regarding intimate encounters and relationships. A DNA and criminal record check can really enlighten one with an epiphany about future partners and spouses.

Heaven and hell are inside our minds, hearts, and souls. Good people are already in heaven, and bad people are in hell. Even before death, one's life is often based on one's being. Goodness is a blessing and brings peace and happiness inside and outside in relationships. Badness is a curse and brings turbulence and troubles, sometimes leading to crimes. Prayer and meditation, obeying law and order, can cure one's soul. The free will of individuals to decide whether to be and live in goodness, happiness, peace, and to abide by and be guided by society's laws is available to everyone. Love is a powerful force, emotion, and energy that can lead to good choices in actions and relationships. Choose love and goodness, and that is heaven on earth; choose hate and badness, and that is hell on earth. Criminals often choose the latter. Living can be heaven or hell, depending on whether one decides to be good or evil!

Heaven and Hell was the seventh modern sonnet book about how being good means going to heaven after physical death, and being bad means hell. Goodness, virtue and laws versus evil, vice and crime in society.

Poem 1: Heaven & Hell

1.	*Our souls' life jour-neys, free to choose <u>vir-tue</u>,*	A
2.	*Pure good-ness, or e-vil cor-rup-tion, <u>vice</u> --*	B
3.	*Ga-ther ex-pe-rien-ces both false or <u>true</u>.*	A
4.	*Foll-ow an an-gel's or dev-il's ad-<u>vice</u>,*	B
5.	*As our hu-man in-stincts form our lost <u>souls</u>.*	C
6.	*Sin's temp-ta-tion and plea-sure can tor-<u>ture</u>*	D
7.	*Us to fore-go in-no-cence. Switch-ing <u>roles</u>*	C
8.	*To gain bad know-ledge, we lose our fu-<u>ture</u>.*	D
9.	*God's pu-nish-ment or re-ward? Re-<u>li-gions</u>*	E
10.	*Re-mind us that past hu-ma-ni-ty <u>fell</u>*	F
11.	*From grace. Which of the spi-ri-tual <u>le-gions</u>*	E
12.	*Will we join? The e-vil ar-mies of H<u>ell</u>*	F
13.	*Or the world God cre-a-ted in s<u>e-ven</u>*	G
14.	*Days, which for good peo-ple may be H<u>ea-ven</u>?*	G

Analysis Poem 1: Heaven & Hell

The Structure of this poem follows a philosophical dialogue with the speaker contemplating the choices between good and evil. The flowing lines maintain a deliberate pacing that mimics deep thought. This pacing creates a sense of weight, as if the speaker is struggling with a profound decision that requires careful deliberation. The absence of a strict rhyme scheme or meter mirrors the uncertainty and openness of the question being asked — the choice between virtue and vice is not predetermined, and the structure leaves space for contemplation. The Meaning of the poem revolves around the human condition and the moral choices that shape one's spiritual journey. The speaker explores the idea of free will — how we can choose between virtue, which aligns with God's creation, or vice, which leads to spiritual corruption. The poem frames these choices within the context of temptation and sin, with the idea of switching roles.

The Imagery in the poem draws heavily on religious symbolism. The references to 'angel's or devil's advice,' 'sin's temptation,' and 'God's punishment or reward' evoke vivid religious iconography. The imagery of 'spiritual legions' and 'fallen grace' serves to remind the reader of the eternal battle between light and darkness, and the consequences of each choice. This eternal struggle reflects the poem's nuanced view of moral conflict — good and evil are not distant, but intrinsic parts of the human soul. Purgatory is an in-between state; on earth, crimes lead to jail.

The Literary devices used include contrast, with the opposites of virtue and vice, and personification, as 'sins' and 'temptations' are depicted almost as active agents. The rhetorical question, 'Which of the spiritual legions / Will we join?' prompts the reader to reflect on their own moral choices. The personification of sin and temptation serves to externalize the moral battle within the individual. The Effect of the poem is thought-provoking. It calls the reader to contemplate about the spiritual path they are on. The effect is not to offer easy answers but to ask profound questions that stir deeper introspection. The poetess is both angel/devil mentally, in between heaven and hell simultaneously.

The Poetess: Believing in a soul inside our bodies is formalized in religions. After physical birth and then death, the body decays, whereas the soul is immortal and continues being and living in the spiritual realms of Earth and the Universe. The brain has the mind, the heart has the emotions, which together are aspects of the soul's memories of experiences and relationships. The body has needs: food, water, air, clothing, shelter, companionship, and for some, sex. Morality, knowing good and evil, and laws and crimes are part of life's lessons to gain knowledge and wisdom. Some are gained through trials and errors, some from formal education, or informal and indirect learning from others. Materialism and greed, while physically alive, can mean reward and success if legally obtained, or punishment and failure if illegally obtained.
I think being aware of good and evil thoughts inside us, along with outside actions, means purgatory is the halfway point...

Poem 10: Mysterious Meeting

Life was lived in a most ordinary

Way, both practical in the day. But dreams

At night led to asking, "Shall we marry

Soon and meet, travel over lands and streams?

Let us promise that we will be lovers."

Thus determined, they crossed the vast distance

To meet their fates. Strange foreboding hovers,

Fed by fears it would not be a romance.

His ship was raided by greedy pirates!

Without her love and support, his tantrum

Exploded! In anger, his note berates

Her to end their future. Sadly, the drum

Beats of their hearts' desires, fed by curious

Urges, had no meeting so mysterious...

Analysis Poem 10: Mysterious Meeting

The Structure of the poem is fluid yet slightly fractured, echoing the ebb and pull of a dreamscape slipping into reality. It begins with symmetry — short, balanced lines that reflect the simplicity of daily life, but soon spills into longer, uneven phrases as the emotional stakes rise. Rhyme appears intermittently, not as a scaffold but as a pulse. This is a poetess unafraid of letting the poem breathe unevenly, from giving way to feeling, and not the other way around. The Meaning centers on the quiet collision between fantasy and consequence. Two lovers live separately yet share a nightly vision of union. They give weight to this longing, chasing it across landscapes, only to find that desire without resilience can unravel. It is not the journey that undoes them, but the fragility of expectation

The Imagery in the poem blurs the border between fairytale and emotional realism. "Lands and streams" suggest an idyllic escape, while 'greedy pirates' intrude like symbols of life's intrusions. The 'drum beats' of desire transform into dirges of disappointment, capturing how passion can shift its tempo when shaken by hardship. The Literary devices are understated but keen. Personification lives in the phrases 'fates' and 'foreboding hovers', giving the journey an almost cosmic weight. There is irony in the poem's arc: what begins as a romantic quest ends with a note of petulance, not poetry. The lovers who vowed togetherness collapse under pressure, undone by the very intensity that once connected them.

The Effect is one of quiet unraveling. The reader is left with a sense of sorrow that does not scream, while the love story dissolves. The poem allows space for ambiguity, trusting the absence of resolution to speak more truthfully than any neat conclusion might. In the end, the most mysterious thing is not the meeting. On the contrary, it is how something so longed for could end so simply, so sadly. This restraint is the poet's most daring gesture: to let yearning echo louder than fulfillment ever could. She recalls that her personal relationships, too, are sadly based on foolish fantasy, not reality.

The Poetess: Telepathy of thoughts and feelings is a theory that occult transmission can be done from one person to another via ESP extra-sensory perception, beyond the 5 physical senses. Lucid dreams can occur in the day or night between people. Lovers, partners, friends, and family sometimes claim they can contact each other remotely and might say,"I was just thinking about you, and you called!" A coincidence or synchronicity between imagination and reality. Intuition is also a way to gauge one's connection in reading subconscious and conscious thoughts and how manifestation in reality can confirm the accuracy of one's sensitivity. Strangers might meet and become friends, partners, lovers, and spouses, starting with dreaming, fantasizing, and a mutual feeling of matching and intimacy upon meeting, wherein attraction leads to compatibility, regardless of similarities or differences. If no meeting occurs, it remains unverified.

Poem 15: Body Parts

A torso, foot, hand, severed by chopping,
Torn apart, bagged, and mailed after murder.
How awful to read bad news while shopping –
Crimes of passion or cold blood. To order
A package and receive a foot by mail,
Or hand, must have cost a lot in postage.
Police and media searched for the young male
Suspect, posting photos until hostage,
Recognized while browsing the internet.
Everyone witnesses by newspapers
Most Wanted criminal suspects who whet
Public attention with evil capers.
Victims who are torn apart, dismembered,
Are sympathized with and thus remembered.

Analysis Poem 15: Body Parts

The structure of this poem is a tight, rhythmic descent, each quatrain progresses with clinical calm, mirroring the cold detachment of news consumption. There is a deliberate contradiction in the tone: the horrifying details are delivered with almost formal grace. The rhyme scheme is steady, grounding the reader even as the subject matter destabilizes. It is a clever constraint; the poem uses order to explore chaos, as if the form itself resists the dismemberment it describes. The Meaning unpacks society's numb familiarity with violence. The horror is not just in the 'severed' body parts; it is reflected in how we absorb this atrocity between errands, mid-scroll, and mid-life. 'How awful to read bad news while shopping' frames the grotesque within the banal. The poem reflects the slow, collective desensitization to crimes within society. The final couplet restores humanity to the victims, but only after the spectacle is complete.

The Imagery is raw and matter-of-fact: 'bagged and mailed', 'a foot by mail', and 'torn apart'. These are headlines, stripped of euphemism. The poetess gives us no veil to hide behind, making the reader complicit in the same voyeurism that fuels media attention. The Literary devices include enjambment that mimics a breathless reaction, and irony that drips from phrases like 'must have cost a lot in postage.' That one line encapsulates the absurdity of our responses — of humor seeping into horror. The poem here weaponizes understatement, not to minimize, but to magnify the grotesque through contrast.

The Effect is unsettling. The reader finishes the poem not with closure but a kind of grim pause. The poetess does not exploit violence for shock, but examines the violence in our detachment. This emotional restraint is chillingly effective because it is exactly how the world reacts to real crime news.

The Poetess: Dismemberment of a human after death might happen for: medical reasons, research or donation, implant surgeries, murder and revenge, or cannibalism. Mail order shopping is so common nowadays because of the internet and websites like: Amazon, Temu, Wish, Shein, Walmart, and packages are delivered directly to doorsteps. The government-regulated public mail and private corporate couriers have laws and policies regarding packages, from the wrapping to handling to delivery. It is even more strict with human body parts. Government, police and the media cooperate when conducting a manhunt for a guilty suspect with a search warrant for arrest, publishing 'Most Wanted' criminals on websites and news articles, plus television reports. If anyone receives such a package, contact 911 Police.
This poem is based on reading about a LGBTQ interracial murder involving a male sex worker and a male student who met online and then in person in Canada 2012. A body torn into its parts -- a sexual synecdoche of the 'most wanted'.

Poem 17: Curse of Nomads

Disturbed by the news, Gyp spread the tarot
Cards for her tribe. "Maybe our lives' fortune
Will show in the cards?" Her tamed pet parrot
Watched from its cage. "Wait, it will end in June."
Coincidence, the Devil and Hangman
Appeared! "Something bad will happen. Power
And poverty are on hold. All Roman
Gypsies overturn destiny. Tower
Inverted." They listened, silent, frightened
By their future. "Who will help lift this curse?
No country to call our home, enlightened
Though we are?" History could not reverse
Their fate as crucifixion witnesses.
"Jesus saves souls." The parrot confesses.

Analysis Poem 17: Curse Of Nomads

The Structure of this poem leans on dialogue and prophecy. The lines fall like shuffled cards — measured, but not mechanical. Rhyme dances lightly, often at the end of a thought rather than in syncopated rhythm, giving the poem a feel of unfolding ritual. The poem captures a mystic rhythm without formal rigidity, like the chant of a people trying to control what cannot be tamed. The Meaning centers on a people haunted by rootlessness and fate. Gyp consults the tarot not for curiosity, but for survival. The cards become a reflection of centuries of exile, warning that even the mystical offers no real refuge. Their question, "Who will help lift this curse?" is not just a spiritual lament, but a historical wound. Even prophecy, it seems, cannot soften the weight of collective memory. The Imagery in the poem blends divination and despair. 'The Devil and Hangman' conjure dread instantly, while 'Tower inverted' signals upheaval that cannot be undone. The parrot, a strange, almost comic detail, becomes the unexpected oracle as its confession ties faith and fate in a single breath. "Jesus saves souls" lands like a ghost-note: part hope, part surrender. The poem parodies the parrot as a prophet of ignorant believers.

The Literary devices include symbolism drawn from the tarot, which the poetess uses as emotional archetypes. The contrast between "power and poverty", between "enlightened" and "no home" paints a cultural identity suspended between knowing and suffering. The parrot's voice is the final, subversive stroke; is it mocking or divine? It is deliberately unclear, adding to the eerie reverberation.

The Effect is one of lingering disquiet, like something whispered through generations. The poem does not plead for sympathy; it speaks from the core of a people who have stopped expecting it. By layering mysticism with historical trauma, the poetess crafts a lament that is both grounded and ghostly. What resonates most is not the fortune itself, but the helplessness of knowing it and still being unable to change it.

The Poetess: Egypt and nomadic gypsies have a reputation for fortune-telling using tarot cards and crystal ball gazing. Predicting the future based on the present situation can provide helpful advice on what to do or not do regarding relationships and transactions -- if their accuracy resonates with the customer and aligns with reality. If a positive or negative outcome is predicted, a person might decide on an action, hoping to attain the desired reaction and goal. Personal, social, professional, and business questions have been asked of psychics and occult practitioners. Considering the money involved, it might be cheaper just to buy one's own occult tools and learn how to use them.
I use occult divination, spiritual protection, and energy vibration healing tools and jewelry: tarot cards, Ouija board, crystal pendulum, stones, tuning fork, frequencies, amulets, pendants, and bracelets. I also consult with professional psychics.

Poem 26: Violent Exit

Calculating that a violent e<u>xit</u>

Would benefit her for life insu<u>rance</u>,

Viola became argumentative. '<u>Sit</u>

And stop walking around.' Near the ent<u>rance</u>

Was the worldly normal life outside <u>jail</u>.

'I could obey and behave because <u>guilt</u>

Can control me. Without freedom through b<u>ail</u>,

I suppose I am trapped by these walls b<u>uilt</u>

For criminals.' Looking around hopel<u>ess</u>

Souls, she wondered which one would try ass<u>ault</u>

And murder her? 'Ignore all the helpl<u>ess</u>

And weak. Find someone mean who will find f<u>ault</u>

With me. Who believes reincar<u>nation</u>

Is better than living in damn<u>ation</u>?'

Analysis Poem 26: Violent Exit

The Structure of the poem is framed like a slow mental unraveling, as each line incrementally pulls us deeper into Viola's fraying sense of control. The rhyme scheme is organized, but like the narrator's logic, it is fractured, hesitant, and compulsive. The enjambments feel deliberate, as if thoughts are too urgent to pause for syntax. The poem does not write madness; it lets us step into its pacing with uncertain, slippery, yet disturbingly clear rhyme. The Meaning revolves around desperation: Viola trapped in a penal space, both literal and existential, calculating her own end as a means to freedom. Her moral decay is a pragmatic weighing of options; if violence equals insurance, then victimhood becomes currency. The narrative dances along the edge of sanity, painting a woman who is both aware and undone by her surroundings.

The Imagery is bleak and institutional: 'walls built for criminals,' 'near the entrance,' 'souls' who are 'helpless.' Even freedom feels contaminated — just 'bail,' not redemption. The suggestion of reincarnation adds a surreal layer, fusing Eastern philosophical escape with Western fatalism. It becomes unclear whether she fears death or demands it as liberation.

The Literary devices include internal monologue and implied irony: Viola's belief that guilt can be a behavioral anchor suggests self-awareness, yet she still seeks her own destruction. The question, 'Who believes reincarnation is better than living in damnation?' does not invite an answer; it just lingers, like a dare. The poem portrays the character not as a victim nor a villain but as both, having experienced imprisonment in isolation and this dilemma -- a morally ambiguous figure staring back.

The Effect is uneasy and tense. The reader is not permitted detachment. There is no catharsis here, only complicity. The poem turns this act of self-sabotage into something intimate, intelligent, and terrifying. It allows Viola the last word, in the form of a spiritual gamble, which is a powerful gesture. Faith becomes both her curse and her only escape hatch.

The Poetess: Imprisonment in a jail is for people who have committed crimes against person or property, decided by courts, Judges, and juries and Police. Criminals might think about serving the years as punishment; thus, they attempt suicide to end their physical lives or trigger a violent incident to be murdered. Hell is a jail cell. Being bad and guilty in jail, trapped with others similar in being, can also be a deep learning experience, changing one inside in repentance or vengeance. Locations that host the same gender: prisons, shelters, convents, monasteries, private Catholic schools, army bases, and police stations. (Pronounce violent as vi'-lent.)

Poem 32: Refugee Rape

Soldiers and rebels compete in battle

During civil conflicts. Animals force

Like bulls mounting to mate docile cattle

Without consent nor marriage. Men's remorse

Could release these women from this torture!

If rape destroys people, persecution

Of rapist and victim kills their future

Marriages. Some prefer execution

To surviving scarred in a rape shelter,

Horrible memories of a victim,

Weaker than a soldier turned torturer.

Why are there no laws to control such whim?

Soldiers without honour. How to escape

Their cold sexuality expressed in rape?

Analysis Poem 32: Refugee Rape

The Structure is formal and unflinching, a fourteen-line sonnet-like container barely holding the horror within. Each quatrain presses forward with tight rhythm, as if the structure is all that separates the poem from chaos. There is no lyrical diversion or soft entry; the first line charges into 'soldiers and rebels', and we are already inside the war. This is a poem which uses form as a shield, not to protect the reader, but to survive the telling. The Meaning centers on sexual violence as both a byproduct and a weapon of war. The comparison to 'bulls mounting...cattle' is not metaphor for shock's sake; it is a brutal stripping of language to its rawest analogy. The poem demands not sympathy, but reckoning. It asks why remorse is rarer than assault, why silence outlives justice, and why laws dissolve under uniforms.

The Imagery in the poem is bestial, not poetic — 'Animals', 'docile cattle', 'shelter', 'scarred', 'whim'. The juxtaposition of 'torture' and 'marriage' disorients, highlighting how war rewrites womanhood not just through harm but through erasure. 'Execution' becomes preferable to survival, not as exaggeration, but rather as bitter reality.

The Literary devices include repetition of interrogatives — 'Why are there no laws?' and 'How to escape?' — forming the moral backbone of the piece. The contrast between 'torturer' and 'turned soldier' blurs the lines of identity: these are not just rogue men; they are institutionalized predators. The poem offers no relief. Her questions just bleed, and her refusal to soften the blow is her most honest craft. The horror of helpless female victims and the men in uniform who use authority to commit sexual crimes!

The Effect is visceral as well as inescapable. The violence is not framed for empathy but for accountability. By naming rape so directly, the poem reclaims what war attempts to erase — dignity through confrontation. The poem ends not with resolution, but with accusation, and that is its integrity.

The Poetess: Refugees of war or natural disasters are sometimes placed in temporary camps until the conflict ends, allowing some to return home or to continue to another country. Stereotypically, females are the rape victims and males are the rapists -- a gender difference that extends to personality, with men being aggressive and women passive. The horror of some camps is that sexual predators: military soldiers and personnel, camp officials and aid workers, smugglers and traffickers, and fellow refugees have the advantage because of the situation of homelessness, hunger, and being foreign in another country. Sex without love and respect occurs because there are no rights for refugees in these camps. Employees should be punished for taking advantage of refugees who are helpless. (Pronounce sexuality as sex-ua-li-ty.)

Poem 36: Stonehenge Solstice

The celebration was in the phallic
Sculptures' ground, consecrated for fertile
Dancing between lovers, an idyllic
Rite. Women and men considered virile,
Danced naked, enjoying Summer solstice.
The hot sun warmed their bodies, a ritual
Where sweating beat medicated poultice,
Releasing toxins, raising spiritual
Energy for the primitives, heathen
In their instincts. Every male erection,
Pointed skyward like the stones to heaven!
Their females stared, circled their direction,
Excited by their bloody sacrifice
Of their pure virginity at sunrise.

Analysis Poem 36: Stonehenge Solstice

The structure of this poem mimics chant and ceremony. It moves like a procession with a classical ABAB pattern that roots its paganism in familiar lyric tradition. Each quatrain spirals deeper into sensual abandon, culminating in the climactic final couplet. The poem builds tension like a priestess orchestrating a rite — sound and sense aligning with precision.

The Meaning explores ancient fertility rituals not as quaint myth, but as a raw celebration of sex, power, and spiritual release. The poem casts no moral judgment; it presents the orgiastic rites as sincere devotion. Solstice becomes both metaphor and medium for human hunger: for pleasure, for transcendence, for godliness through flesh.
The Imagery is lush and tactile — 'phallic sculptures', 'sweating', 'erection', 'bloody sacrifice'. These are not symbolic stand-ins; they are literal invocations. Nature and body are indistinct; the sun warms their nakedness. Erection and stone mirror each other, suggesting that even architecture yearns.

The Literary devices include fertility symbolism in the 'phallic / Sculptures ground' sustained religious imagery ('rite', 'sacrifice') that frames sexuality as ritual, and sharp juxtaposition between 'pure virginity' and 'bloody sacrifice', highlighting the tension between sanctity and violence. The final lines build crescendo through structure, not just content. There is genius in how the poem allows the sacred and the carnal to exist without contradiction. How polite and civilized it now is in contrast...

The Effect is liberating, unnerving, and strangely reverent. The poem returns ritual to its primal function, confronting the instincts we bury under civilization. It leaves the reader flushed, not from scandal, but from recognition. It dares you to feel what those dancers felt: raw, alive, and utterly mortal. What is most shocking is not the nudity or the sexuality, but how unashamed it all is!

The Poetess: Ancient architecture can be interpreted by modern archaeology through various theories of its function -- shelter, ceremony, religion, etc. Stonehenge is a mysterious configuration of vertical stone pillars (phallic) in a circular arrangement (vulvic). Speculation has linked it to a calendar, solar clock, burial, cremation ground, and cultural ceremonies of Celtic, Wiccan, and Druid pagan fertility rituals. Based on its continued popularity for marriages and nature celebrations, it probably did have a multifunctional purpose for couples and communities celebrating outdoors in a natural yet man-made setting -- such as Beltane May Day, with maypole ribbon dancing and hand-fasting -- tying the knot as a couple in the United Kingdom.

Poem 49: Demon Children

Medication caused a disori*ented*
Feeling. Thinking she heard evil v*oices*
Whispering in her home, a torm*ented*
Thought controlled her to exorcise n*oises*.
Her children, scared, stared at her glare, po*ssessed*
By anger. "Get out, go away, d*evil!*"
She shouted at her children, so ob*sessed*
To baptize them, eliminate *evil*
Which entered them. Despite their unc*ertain*
Faces, she carried one by one, sc*reaming*
To the tub. "At last, your final c*urtain*
Will end your evil innocence, d*reaming*
Of the Beast, living turned sour as *lemons*."
She then submerged and strangled her d*emons!*

Analysis Poem 49: Demon Children

The Structure of this poem presses forward in clipped, almost breathless lines — short clauses stacked one after another like the shallow, panicked breaths of its protagonist. The rhyme scheme runs tightly, but it does not smooth the reading; instead, it tightens the grip, holding the reader inside the frantic sequence of events. The poem understands that control in form can heighten chaos in content — restraint and frenzy feeding each other.

The Meaning is stark: a mother's medicated haze warps into a religiously tinged delusion, turning love into lethal violence. As her perception fractures, 'evil voices' blur into her children's innocence. She baptizes them not for salvation, but for execution, reflecting a chilling inversion of the sacred.

The Imagery here is intimate and horrifying. The domestic space — home and tub — becomes an arena for exorcism. 'Final curtain' and 'evil innocence' play with opposites, hinting at her inability to distinguish purity from corruption. 'Sour as lemons' is a small but startling sensory note, grounding the surreal in the mundane.

The Literary devices include irony in the inversion of baptism, repetition in 'devil,' and personification of evil as something inhabiting her children's bodies. The enjambment between 'strangled her / demons' breaks at exactly the point where reality fractures, as children become 'demons' in her mind.

The Effect is deeply unsettling. What stays is not the act itself, but the calm inevitability with which she carries it out. The poetess does not shout horror at the reader; she whispers it, and that quiet is what lingers. It is a portrayal of madness that does not sensationalize; it simply lets it stand, unbearably close.

The Poetess: Water baptism for Christians reenacts the purification and entry into the religion, which can occur as a child or as an adult. Children are thought to be born innocent, but gradually gain knowledge and experience, losing their innocence and ignorance. Killing someone bad versus killing someone good is a decision made by killers or police, and unfortunately, sometimes by family in domestic murder. Thoughts feelings, and actions can be right or wrong, or confused with both. How to tell if one's own judgment is true and valid or false and invalid regarding others' goodness or badness? Drugs and paranoia can lead to confused reasoning -- hearing voices in the head inciting one to harm oneself or others. This is based on a true horror murder story from Texas 2001 about a mother who killed her children, thinking they were possessed by demons inside, even though she herself was either possessed by a demon or insane with schizophrenia.

Poem 50: Soul's Corruption

Mulling on life and its mor*ality*,

"Goodness rewards, but if an il*legal*

Act is committed, the soul's qu*ality*

Corrodes. Obedience toward the *legal*

Guidelines is safer for goals. Although c*rime*

Can achieve them with vices, not vir*tues.*"

In the mirror, she observed. "Hiding g*rime*

Behind makeup, will I have to pay *dues*

When caught someday? Will God and man pu*nish*

Me for lying and hiding a*ttempted*

Murder of spouse? Will society ba*nish*

A wife who cheated her husband, *tempted*

By his wealth? For his life's inter*ruption*

Would mean imprisonment by cor*ruption!*"

Analysis: Poem 50: Soul's Corruption

The Structure is methodical, mirroring the speaker's own moral inventory. The rhyme moves predictably, like the careful circling of a guilty mind that refuses to stumble. Lines are neatly packed, but their regularity feels like a mask, like a measured voice concealing roiling thought. Even the rhythm feels rehearsed, as though recounting wrongdoing was practiced in private. The poetess' craft mirrors the character's psychology: control as cover and form as camouflage for moral decay.

The Meaning pivots on self-reflection gone rancid. The speaker knows the moral law, acknowledges divine justice, yet openly weighs crime as a viable tool for personal gain. Her infractions — infidelity and attempted murder — are laid out not for confession but for calculation. There is no intent to change, only to assess whether the benefits outweigh the risks.

The Imagery rests on concealment: "hiding grime behind makeup" becomes the central metaphor for deception, suggesting both physical disguise and moral cover-up. The mirror is both witness and accomplice, reflecting a curated surface that edits out corruption. Even her own face becomes part of the crime scene, an object to manipulate for survival. The Literary devices include rhetorical questions that double as self-interrogation and foreshadowing. Irony threads the piece: her awareness of 'corruption' does not halt her path; it sharpens her cunning. Symbolism in "pay dues" blends legal and spiritual judgment, showing her dual fear of God and society.

The Effect is claustrophobic. We are not outside judging her; we are locked in her own mental courtroom, watching her defend herself to herself. The poem's refusal to offer moral resolution turns the piece into an open wound, a confession without repentance. This is guilt weaponized as strategy, not as conscience — an unsettling portrait of a soul that knows the truth yet prefers the shadows. The wife leaves the readers hanging on whether murdering a husband for money is worth the imprisonment and corruption of her soul. The poetess remains single without worrying about such decisions.

The Poetess: Internal dialogues voiced aloud alone, including possible crimes, are done as in Shakespearean monologue soliloquies. Murdering a spouse for his money while cheating on him in adultery is a heavy decision that might either prevent it or plot it. If caught, it would be categorized as first-degree premeditated murder with a motive, such as wealth and exchanging a spouse for a lover. Either mariticide, the killing of a husband, or uxoricide, the killing of a wife, in domestic murder statistics is done by an intimate partner not necessarily in marriage. There are more female victims 34% than male 6% with a ratio of 5:1. Divorce is probably a better option for couples who are no longer committed to their marriage and have joint property to distribute, including those in LGBTQ adultery affairs.

Poem 79: Black Friday Thirteenth

Superstitions about Friday thirteenth
Are based on various theories: Christian –
Jesus arrested by soldiers on hint
From Judas to Rome's Empire, serpentine
Intentions hidden in Gethsemane
Garden, not Eden. Apostles, the twelve
Trusted, with one bribed by silver money
Revealing secretly where they did delve
In prayer with Jesus – the odd number.
Crucified, his mortal life then ended
Tortured by guards. Disciples in slumber
Unaware, when the Lord had depended
On them for support. Death on Black Friday –
Hung as the thirteenth man that tragic day.

Analysis Poem 79: Black Friday Thirteenth

The Structure is orderly and almost historical in tone, unfolding like a lesson retold with a controlled rhyme anchoring it. The pacing is deliberate, as though reciting an inherited story passed down through generations, each retelling polishing the moral weight. The poem shapes superstition into narrative, allowing faith and folklore to share the same frame, refusing to separate sacred belief from cultural myth. The Meaning traces the superstition's Christian roots, from betrayal in Gethsemane to crucifixion. The 'thirteenth' becomes not a mere numeral but a symbolic fracture, a curse born of abandonment, greed, and the collapse of loyalty. By rooting the superstition in betrayal, the poem reframes it from irrational fear to inherited memory, one that still haunts the cultural imagination. High-rise building elevators still omit numbering the 13th floor because of this.

The Imagery is biblical yet localized: 'serpentine intentions' entwines betrayal with Eden's first deception, layering the narrative with the sense that treachery is as old as humanity. 'Bribed by silver money' conjures the glint of coins that weigh more than loyalty, while 'the odd number' becomes a quiet emblem of imbalance.

The Literary devices include allusion, symbolic numerology, and the juxtaposition of sacred spaces (Eden, Gethsemane) to suggest that betrayal is not bound to a single place or moment. The irony of 'disciples in slumber' shows the human tendency to fail at the very moment one's loyalty matters most. Enjambment keeps the momentum unbroken, like the inevitability of the Passion narrative moving toward its conclusion.

The Effect is solemn and unyielding. The superstition is no longer quaint -- it becomes a compressed theology of betrayal and loss, history reframed as omen. By closing on 'the thirteenth man', the poetess denies us release. It is a reminder that the myths we treat lightly may have been born from blood, and that some fears are simply the residue of wounds too deep to heal.

The Poetess: Triskaidekaphobia is the fear of the number 13. In the Christian Bible, Jesus (Quran Issa / Talmud Yeshu) was the 13th man with 12 disciples: Andrew, Bartholomew, James (Zebedee's son), James (Alphaeus' son), John, Matthew, Philip, Simon (the Zealot), Simon Peter, Thaddaeus, Thomas, and Judas Iscariot. Jesus was crucified on a Friday before the Jewish Sabbath -- thus the superstition of misfortune associated with Friday the 13th. Thus, Good Friday, also known as Black Friday, Holy Saturday, and Easter Sunday, is linked to this superstition. Modern-day shopping in Canada and America also uses the label Black Friday for the start of Christmas shopping after Thanksgiving Thursday.

Poem 105: Ramadan Reverie

Years ago, spiritual revelation
Was revealed to Mohammad. The Qur'an
Was a guide for the soul's elevation,
Read in Mecca, Medina, to Tehran.
In Cave of Hira, Night of Destiny
Foretold the meaning and purpose of Man,
Observing a lifestyle of scrutiny
By Allah, educating each human.
Angel Jibril inspired his reverie,
Enlightening his views, meditating
In Medina with his delivery.
The verses inspire without dictating
In chapters read by Islam's followers.
Its intended goal raises, not lowers.

Analysis Poem 105: Ramadan Reverie

The Structure is deliberate, unfolding in evenly measured rhyme that mirrors the steady rhythm of sacred recitation. Each couplet stands contained yet linked, like beads on a prayer string, creating both continuity and contemplation. This orderly progression reflects the subject's devotion. The poem's form mirrors the internal order of faith, where repetition becomes a form of worship. The Meaning lies in the act of recalling a foundational spiritual revelation and its transmission through history into modern devotion. The narrative moves from the moment of divine contact — marked by the presence of an angel — to the enduring life of those words among believers. The text's role is not to command, but to guide, offering elevation of the soul rather than coercion.

The Imagery is rooted in sacred geography and prophetic vision: the 'Cave of Hira' becomes both a physical and spiritual birthplace; the 'Night of Destiny' glows with transformative power. Named cities — Mecca, Medina, and Tehran map the expansion of belief, linking history to contemporary practice. Islam is also second to Christianity in the population of believers of world religions.

The Literary devices at work include allusion to scriptural history, personification of the divine message as an 'educator,' and parallelism in naming holy sites to emphasize faith's reach. The tone avoids imperatives, reflecting its own line about inspiration that 'inspires without dictating.'

The effect is meditative. Rather than trying to persuade, it invites the reader to enter the contemplative rhythm of devotion, mirroring the experience of recitation. The closing sentiment, 'raises not lowers,' leaves the reader with an upward gaze, carrying a suggestion of spiritual ascent beyond the page. The poem offers not a narrative arc of conflict and resolution, but a sustained stillness, where the weight is in the memory of revelation itself. It is a work that positions faith not as a demand but as an atmosphere, and in doing so, makes space for the reader's own quiet engagement.

The Poetess: Three religions -- Judaism, Islam, and Christianity have common ancestors written about in their different books: the Torah/ Talmud, Quran/ Tafsir, and Bible. There are Prophets in the holy books inspired by God to follow certain laws toward being good, wherein one's soul within one's body will align with God and goodness. However, often humanity has both good and evil, along with free will, to choose one's thoughts and actions. Ramadan is a month of fasting to commemorate this historical event, when Prophet Muhammad was inspired by revelation from the angel Jibril / Gabriel as a guide for mankind. It starts with a crescent moon on the lunar calendar, and Eid al-Fitr breaks the fast with feasting.

Poem 107: Inferno Infinity

In Hell, suffering in inf<u>inity</u>

With everyone evil in their spir<u>its</u>,

Hopeless belief in Holy Tr<u>inity</u>

Long forgotten, the bad nightmare vis<u>its</u>

Of sinners may trigger epi<u>phany</u>.

All evil crimes, from murder to ass<u>ault</u>

And diseases groaning caco<u>phony</u>.

People kill or be killed, guilty at <u>fault</u>.

No one cares for virtues, only <u>vices</u>.

Troubles have neither right nor wrong con<u>science</u>

Because all are sinners. One ad<u>vises</u>

On how to bring destruction without <u>sense</u>.

Souls remain imprisoned in infer<u>no</u> --

Thoughts, words, actions, evil as they all <u>know</u>.

Analysis Poem 107: Inferno Infinity

The structure is tight and contained, mirroring the prison-like quality of the setting it describes. Its rhyme is irregular but still patterned, creating a sense of order that clashes with the chaos of Hell — an intentional tension that mirrors the paradox of eternal punishment. The pacing moves quickly line to line, as if the damned have no room to pause or breathe. The poem's construction feels like a corridor that only narrows the further you walk. The Meaning centers on a vision of Hell as both eternal and self-perpetuating. There is no divine intervention here. Suffering is presented not merely as retribution but as an environment in which evil becomes the only currency, and morality is absent from all transactions. The speaker's tone is observational, yet without offering escape or hope, which deepens the horror.

The Imagery is visceral and auditory — 'groaning cacophony' not only evokes pain but also suggests the constant noise of torment, while 'kill or be killed' conjures a lawless battlefield. The environment is less fiery than psychological, with Hell defined by the presence of vice and the absence of virtue. Disease and violence form a bleak collage of degradation.

The Literary devices include irony (epiphany arriving too late to save), alliteration 'sense. / Souls', and juxtaposition between religious language 'Holy Trinity' and the brutality of crime. The list of sins functions almost as a litany, replacing sacred prayer with a catalogue of human failings.

The Effect is suffocating. It invites the reader into a place where moral categories collapse, and where the eternal is not divine but corrosive. By refusing any hint of redemption, the poem forces us to dwell in the permanence of corruption, turning 'infinity' from an abstract idea into a felt sentence. We leave the lines carrying the weight of a place that has no exit — not even through thought. Wherever there is evil, is hell.

The Poetess: Inside every person might be good and evil thoughts and feelings that lead to actions. The realization that people are more bad than good can be horrible because harming, not helping, each other would be the standard of behavior. Love, peace, and happiness usually come with goodness -- hate, war, and despondency with badness. On Earth, while still physically and materially bound, since there are civilized laws, people who are bad enough to commit crimes can be caught and put in jail with other evil people. Harming a person or property is usually the goal to gain control over another person. Corrupted individuals infect others and thus must be avoided like a disease that spreads. Prison protects good society by removing bad people from continuing their harm to others. They might repent and change their ways. In the eternal afterlife, people who are bad supposedly go to hell, the good to heaven, and those in between to purgatory. If everyone were bad, committing crimes against each other, Attorney Amelia Alias might decide all parties guilty. There would be no one good to protect as a victim. Hell would be a prison with criminals harming each other in turn.

Poem 122: Outside the War Rages

"Just outside our windows, the war rages,
As men`s moods, full of anger and violence."
"Wars are meant to release men from cages."
"We will read the news from camera lens
Capturing the action of the air bombs
Dropped from planes by military soldiers
And pilots." "Buildings become catacombs
Burying dead. . .lifting weight from shoulders,
Fatigued by living." "Man`s mortality
Ends by beliefs. There are no safe shelters
To protect us from the totality."
"Our houses in cities lay in shatters.
We become squatters for an assassin,
Fatally punishing us for a sin."

Analysis Poem 122: Outside The War Rages

The structure is dialogic, composed of interwoven voices that trade lines as if in a collective lament. Each quoted fragment feels like a shard of conversation overheard in a war zone, the irregular rhyme mirroring the unpredictability of conflict. The stanzas move like flashes of news footage — brief, sharp, and broken — conveying how war shatters both time and thought. The structure itself mimics rubble: phrases intact yet scattered.

The Meaning focuses on the inescapability of war and the collapse of normal life under its weight. The speakers recognize war not only as physical destruction but as a dismantling of beliefs and safety. Their comments carry both resignation and bitter observation: war is framed as something that might 'release men from cages,' but the reality described is entrapment in fear, ruin, and death.

The Imagery is starkly visual — 'buildings become catacombs' transforms civilian architecture into mass graves, while 'camera lens' draws attention to the mediated way many experience war, as distant viewers. The contrast between inside 'our windows' and outside 'the war rages' creates a fragile boundary that feels doomed to break. The Literary devices include metaphor 'houses… lay in shatters' as a stand-in for societal collapse, personification — war as an 'assassin', and irony, the idea that war frees men, even as it imprisons them in destruction. The recurring direct speech blurs the boundary between narrator and victim, turning the reader into a listener to real-time testimony.

The Effect is haunting. We are drawn into the war not as soldiers or generals, but as civilians who cannot flee. The multiplicity of voices denies the comfort of a single, stable narrator; instead, we inhabit a chorus of survival and loss. The closing image of being 'punished for a sin' leaves the conflict's origins deliberately vague, emphasizing the indiscriminate cruelty of war. By the end, we are left not with political analysis, but with the endurance of those who live under falling bombs. Those who thought the war raged outside, viewed remotely via media cameras, photos, and news, would somehow eventually experience the devastation of bombs destroying their own houses and murder by bullets.

The Poetess: Wars can bring out the animal instincts in people to survive or to seek revenge. Looking at historical wars, if it were possible to read from all sides their rationalizations for participating in them, the photos and videos show hell on earth. Often, men being territorial fight the wars, destroy other men's structures, and kill each other as enemies. Weapons can kill people and destroy properties. Women are often victims in war, raped by men who are foreign soldiers or guards. Wars bring out the worst behavior in men, unfortunately. The media try to photograph, write, and record the events for reporting to the public and to outsiders reading and watching the news from a distance. It has been over 80 years since World War 2 ending in 1945, and world peace is certainly better for global progress. (Pronounce violence as vi'-lence.)

Poem 123: Force Majeure Clause

Acts of God, known natural disasters:
Hurricanes, floods, earthquakes, and volcanic
Eruptions, a clause in contracts quite terse
Despite its weight. Sinking the Titanic
Whether done by iceberg or torpedo
Has no insurance liability.
Believers of the Apostles' Credo
And agnostics point culpability
To God or man. Determining degrees:
Purpose, knowing, recklessness, negligence
Based on mental state leads to Judge`s decrees.
Contracting Parties with due diligence
On investigation can state obvious
Findings, but are exempt from oblivious.

Analysis Poem 123: Force Majeure Clause

The Structure of the poem is built on clauses rather than rhythms, each line unfolding like a stipulation in a legal brief. Its tight rhyme and measured rhythm give it the air of a document rather than a confession or lyric. This formality distances the speaker, almost making the poem read like a court transcript. This is a rare maneuver; the poetry inside the framework of law, revealing that structure can feel like a cage as much as a container. The Meaning of the poem spirals around accountability, exposing the tension between divine will and human fault. When the Titanic sinks — whether by iceberg or torpedo — the debate shifts from tragedy to liability. The 'Force Majeure Clause' becomes a symbol of human attempts to codify fate. The poem questions whether calamities are God's interventions or failures of human foresight, leaving the reader in the gray zone where belief, doubt, and responsibility blur together.

The Imagery, though minimal, is precise. Words like 'hurricanes', 'floods', and 'volcanic eruptions' conjure uncontrollable nature, but they appear framed not in awe but in legal restraint. Even the 'Titanic', usually mythologized in cinematic grief, is reduced to a test case in liability. The imagery deliberately strips grandeur from catastrophe, presenting disaster as data points in an insurance ledger. De-mythologizing is intentional; the poem transforms spectacle into document, leaving the emotional residue to seep in through absence. The Literary devices here include irony, stark in its contrast between calamity and clause. The poem uses juxtaposition: sublime forces of nature set against the cold compression of 'due diligence' and 'investigation'. Even the phrase 'exempt from oblivious' bends language into paradox, hinting at how law shields from liability and moral clarity.

The Effect of the poem is one of unsettling detachment. Readers are forced to witness how language designed to protect also erases. Catastrophe, refracted through this lens, becomes depersonalized; yet that very reduction is what stings most. This refusal to grant catharsis is telling; the poem trusts silence and omission as tools, forcing the audience to confront the inhumanity beneath systems meant to safeguard.

The Poetess: Natural disasters caused by God or creation, or wars by humans, are often so major and unforeseeable in their destruction that insurance and business contracts avoid liability for compensating their damages. They would go bankrupt. Ancient religious beliefs sometimes equated certain natural disasters with punishment from God for human evil. The Flood by water and Sodom and Gomorrah by fire are examples of natural disasters that decimated the people and destroyed the properties in those areas. Causes and effects are nowadays scientifically based, but the religious terms remain in use in insurance and contracts. If God caused them as punishment to humanity for evil corruption, too many claims would be impossible to fulfill anyway, and companies would go bankrupt. Any judge, whether a human in court or God in the universe, might base the decision on evidence and testimony, or unprovable and difficult to blame the guilty.

Poem 125: Native Christianity

From ships, the priests arrived to bless na<u>tives</u>
With baptism, teaching ways of the Cr<u>oss</u>,
Hard-earned suffering, unlike that of <u>thieves</u>
Who steal without working, causing a <u>loss</u>.
Through schools and hospitals, edu<u>cation</u>
Taught material and spiritual pro<u>gress</u>
Attained by learning trade and vo<u>cation</u>.
Thousands of years, despite a war's re<u>gress</u>
In World War Two, the great rice te<u>rraces</u>
Remain to feed. Holy Na<u>tivity</u>
And religion blessed some foreign <u>races</u>
With prosperity and fes<u>tivity</u>.
Tribal tradition and Christi<u>anity</u>
Combine skilled pride with humble <u>vanity</u>.

Analysis Poem 125: Native Christianity

The Structure of the poem runs like a chronicle, unspooling in sequential fragments that echo both sermon and report. Each line feels clipped, almost ledger-like, as though recording milestones in the meeting of two worlds. The rhythm does not chase elegance but steadiness, imitating the march of history as it is told by victors rather than participants. Here the poem makes a choice: abandon musical flourish to mirror the institutional tone of colonial records. The Meaning emerges through this recounting of missionary arrival, where baptism, education, and hospitals are framed as gifts bestowed upon native communities. The narrative traces how Christianity entwines itself with local life, linking spiritual salvation with material advancement. Yet beneath the surface, there is ambivalence as the suffering is 'hard-earned', the terraces endure through war, and tradition lingers even as religion spreads.

The Imagery is dual in nature: biblical symbols like the 'Cross' and 'Holy Nativity' collide with concrete markers of livelihood such as 'rice terraces' and 'trade and vocation.' These juxtapositions create a layered tableau where sacred and earthly life converge. Rather than lush description, the imagery works through contrast, drawing its force from the uneasy coexistence of ritual and sustenance. The poem denies sentimental ornament to highlight how cultures mesh in practical, often unspectacular ways. The Literary devices rest on irony and juxtaposition. Words like 'bless' and 'progress' carry double edges, simultaneously sincere and suspect. The terraces act as enduring symbols of native resilience, while festivity reflects how foreign faith reshaped celebration. Even the closing gesture — tradition and Christianity in 'skilled pride' — is ambiguous: is this harmonious blending, or a compromise forged under duress? The poetess sharpens devices into instruments of tension rather than clarity, ensuring the reader feels the unresolved weight.

The Effect of the poem is contemplative unease. Readers are invited to see how colonization cloaked itself in charity, binding salvation to civilization. The voice lingers in the space of ambivalence, neither condemning nor praising fully. The poem allows history's contradictions to stand intact, refusing to reduce complexity into moral absolutes -- that refusal is its quiet power.

The Poetess: Referring to the Philippines, its 'great rice terraces', as another Christianized nation by Europeans; the spiritual conversion also brought education and material development: churches, schools, hospitals, and trades. The majority of natives and mixed-blood individuals are Christian Catholic and combine tribal customs with religious celebrations. Easter and Christmas are popular holidays, and food like roast pig (lechon) and star-shaped shell lanterns (parol) are part of the blending of Southeast Asian, European, and American influences.
My family claims to be of mixed-blood generations back: Moroccan Berber, Spanish Moor, Chinese, and Filipino.

Poem 143: Conviction By Principle

Unexplained misfortune by principle,

Were works of the Devil. Prosecution

In courts, from special evidence, ripple

Through the community. Persecution

Follows the accused, not invincible

With Satan's protection, torture, trials,

Tests and testimonies to crucible

Burning or beheading. Healing vials

That poison or kill, masked in delicious

Potions, evidence for accusation

Soon end another neighbor's malicious

Intent. Their deaths brought peaceful cessation

To some diseases. Public conviction

By death was the town's way of eviction.

Analysis Poem 143: Conviction By Principle

The Structure of the poem resembles a trial transcript, each line a clause of evidence or judgment. Rather than flowing with lyrical grace, it advances with the severity of legal proceedings, dragging the reader from accusation to execution. The rhythm feels procedural, mirroring how communities codify suspicion into law. Here, the poem chooses austerity over flow, showing how form can mimic the cold machinery of persecution. The Meaning exposes the collapse of principle into paranoia. Misfortune is attributed to the Devil, allowing fear to masquerade as justice. Courts, testimonies, and torture become instruments not of truth but of hysteria, where even 'healing vials' or 'delicious potions' are reinterpreted as evidence of guilt. The deaths that follow are chillingly described as 'peaceful cessation,' revealing how violence is rationalized as remedy. The poem interrogates how societies, when blinded by conviction, can transform belief into cruelty.

The Imagery is spare but sharp. 'Burning or beheading' provides blunt violence; 'poison masked in delicious potions' fuses temptation with betrayal. Such images resist ornament, instead confronting the reader with scenes stripped of mercy. Even the phrase 'peaceful cessation' is an intentional distortion, evoking comfort where horror belongs. This calculated restraint ensures the reader feels the cruelty without disguise. The Literary devices lean on irony and inversion. Healing becomes killing, faith becomes persecution, and principle devolves into paranoia. Alliteration in 'tests and testimonies to crucible' heightens the ritual monotony of accusation. The rhyme scheme reinforces inevitability, binding the poem to a pattern as rigid as the trials it depicts. The poetess sharpens devices not for beauty but for indictment, refusing to grant the comfort of lyric excess.

The Effect is unsettling in its detachment. By refusing catharsis, the poem leaves readers in the claustrophobic grip of communal judgment. Conviction here is not justice but eviction, and that inversion lingers as the true punishment. This is the poetess' restraint at its boldest — trusting ambiguity and discomfort to do the lasting work of revelation.

The Poetess: In the infamous witch trials in Salem, Massachusetts, courts were a historical and hysterical example of how a village believed young girls' testimonies -- blaming their mysterious illnesses on adults suspected of practising witchcraft. The Puritanical religious attitude and belief that Satan and his workers can punish people with diseases or disasters, along with the economic class differences wherein most of the accused and accusers were from the lower-income class, formed the foundation of prejudice that led to accusations, investigations, trials, jail torture, confessions, judgments, guilty convictions, and executions by hanging. Young girls, the accusers, versus old women, the accused, and their testimonies express another prejudice by age -- youth against the elderly. Ditto gender bias against women.

Poem 158: Bokor's Zombie

Praying to Bondye using a Vo*dou*
Ritual, Bokor asked Lwas for a zom*bie*.
"My wife has died! Without her, what to *do*?
She cooked and cleaned, working hard as a *bee*!
She was my Mambo, helping custo*mers*
With ailments and healing their dis*eases*."
The Lwas looked at his deeds: the heart mur*murs*
Sent to rivals of jealous mates, *teases*
To separate them. Deciding his sp*ells*
Helped unite spouses, they granted pray*ers*
To revive his wife. Rejoicing, his *yells*
Opened her shut eyes. The funeral h*earse*
Stopped on its way to the ceme*tery*.
How she revived remains a mys*tery*!

Analysis Poem 158: Bokor's Zombie

The Structure of the poem unfolds like a folktale retold in legal verse, with each line both testimony and incantation. The rhythm is steady, moving step by step from grief to ritual, from prayer to miracle. Unlike lyrical effusion, the form keeps its distance, mimicking the measured style of oral storytelling passed down in fragments. This restraint is deliberate; the poem channels tradition's pacing, allowing narrative weight to replace embellishment. The Meaning hinges on grief transmuted into ritual. A husband, unable to bear his wife's death, turns to Vodou, invoking the Loas for return. His reasoning is tender yet practical: she cooked, cleaned, healed, and guided. But beneath the devotion lies ambiguity; his past spells meddled in relationships, not purely benevolent. His request is granted, not simply for love, but because his magic once restored unions.

The Imagery blends the domestic with the supernatural. "She cooked and cleaned, working hard as a bee" grounds the wife in humble labor, while 'opened her shut eyes' offers resurrection without grandeur. Even the halted 'funeral hearse' is practical, a civic interruption to cosmic mystery. The juxtaposition of ordinary service with divine intervention creates a register both intimate and eerie. The poem's choice to veil horror in domestic imagery is subtle.

The Literary devices turn on irony and inversion. Death itself is paused, 'stopped on its way', as if mortality were negotiable. The rhyme scheme highlights inevitability, while the closing couplet leaves uncertainty: 'How she revived remains a mystery!' This final exclamation destabilizes certainty, reminding us that explanations fail where faith and fear intermingle. The poem thrives in ambiguity, wielding devices to question rather than resolve.

The Effect is uncanny and unresolved. Readers are left between awe and unease, unsure whether to celebrate reunion or fear the cost of tampering with death. The poem resists closure, trusting ambiguity to carry the haunting afterlife long after the lines end.

The Poetess: Vodou is a Caribbean religion wherein Bondye (French Bon Dieu for Good God) the supreme God, has spirit helpers -- Lwas who help human beings who sacrifice animals and offerings to them. A warlock bokor can create a zombi, a revived dead person as a slave under his control. Religion and spiritual practices influence believers but can also affect non-believers and outsiders in the interconnectedness of the spiritual electromagnetic energy within bodies and the collective consciousness of thoughts in brains and emotions in hearts, which control physical actions. The inside controls the outside, from interior to exterior. Occult shops sell oils, candles, herbs, crystals, stones, amulets, and cards for rituals.

Poem 169: Kama Sutra Manual

Vatsyayana wrote a book in Sanskrit:
A philosopher whose view of sexual
Union positions to reach the spirit;
Fantasies were written into textual
Passages by experts; introduction
On society, its goals, households, classes,
And the types of women for seduction
Or marriage or harem. With eyeglasses,
Men can read and learn, gain experiences,
With loose women of different countries,
Until they break down a girl's defences,
Her heart and virginity. To increase
Knowledge, read this ancient Hindu tantra,
Practise positions with yogic mantra.

Analysis Poem 169: Kama Sutra Manual

The Structure of the poem is archival, moving like an index through categories rather than unfolding as free-flowing lyric. The rhythm mirrors the didactic tone of manuals, less interested in poetry's music than in its capacity to codify. The poem borrows the dry symmetry of catalogues, using the shape of instruction to interrogate the act of instruction itself. The Meaning dwells on the paradox of codifying desire. What begins as a spiritual guide to union — the pursuit of the spirit through the body — quickly collapses into conquest, seduction, and exploitation. The manual is framed as a tool for men to pursue power: learning, defense-breaking, and possession. The tension lies in whether such systematization of intimacy ennobles or corrupts, and whether knowledge enhances love or reduces it to acquisition.

The Imagery shifts between the austere and the sensual. 'With eyeglasses, / Men can read and learn' places the text in modernity's study, while 'break down a girl's defences, / Her heart and virginity' exposes the raw violence beneath learned sophistication. The juxtaposition of yogic mantra with sexual practice heightens unease, forcing the sacred and the carnal into a single frame. The poem makes imagery a site of fracture. What should elevate is contaminated by what exploits.

The Literary devices rely on irony and juxtaposition. Classical wisdom collides with colonial echoes — 'loose women of different countries' — as knowledge becomes license rather than discipline. The closing couplet pairs 'tantra' with 'mantra,' echoing rhyme while highlighting contradiction: is this spiritual ascent or indulgence masquerading as ritual? The poetic craft here is subversive. Devices serve not to embellish, but to unravel the very authority of the text being invoked. The Effect is one of ambivalence, laced with discomfort. Readers are left to question whether this codification of intimacy can ever escape its shadows of domination. The poem resists judgment, and this refusal to resolve is its strength. The poem entrusts the reader with unease, the mark of a work intent on questioning rather than consoling.

The Poetess: In India, currently the most populated country with 1.45 billion, there is a sex and love manual that has been translated from Sanskrit into English and French. It is the first sex education guide, written in India 3rd century by Vatsyayana Mallanaga. Its chapters are: an introduction classifying society, amorous advances of sexual interest and union, courtship and choosing a wife, married life, adultery, prostitution, and occult attraction. Various positions for sexual intercourse are similar to yoga asana positions. Sex education, if taught in schools, would be useful for learning through books and lectures without having to experience it by trial and error, within or without relationships. Intimacy in the physical, emotional, and mental areas of relationships can extend to sexual -- the more knowledge one has, the more prepared and improved those aspects are. Love with sex is the goal for romantic relationships, along with marriage and happiness.

Poem 186: God's Inspiration

"After the session, I realized ta<u>lent</u>

Is a gift from God!" The tongue of ser<u>pent</u>

And Satan is knowing, but evil, <u>lent</u>

To humans to lose innocence. Re<u>pent</u>

Now and be humbled. The male voice whis<u>pered</u>,

"Gnosis... the source is a secret un<u>known</u>

By most." "Maybe twitters from a small <u>bird</u>?

Or dead male soul?" "To remain unbe<u>known</u>

Would waste it. One must share and enter<u>tain</u>

The public. Within the words is Wis<u>dom</u>.

Prepare yourself! Our meeting is cer<u>tain</u>."

The poetess walked. Tears from God's Kin<u>dom</u>

Rained down on her artist's per<u>spiration</u>,

Humbled by the divine in<u>spiration</u>!

Analysis Poem 186: God's Inspiration

The Structure of the poem unfolds like dialogue embedded within revelation, alternating between quoted speech and reflective narration. Rather than moving in smooth lyrical arcs, it progresses in layered exchanges. The rhythm is fragmented, as if a divine message were filtering through human vessels, incomplete yet insistent. The poem here bends form into conversation, letting interruption and pause embody the nature of revelation itself. The Meaning wrestles with the origin of talent. Is creativity a divine gift, a serpent's temptation, or secret gnosis passed through hidden voices? The poem frames artistic calling as both burden and grace: a test of humility as much as a channel of expression. By placing the speaker between God, Satan, and mysterious whispers, the poem resists simple attribution, insisting that inspiration is contested ground.

The Imagery moves between sacred and ordinary. 'Tears from God's Kingdom' raining onto 'artist's perspiration' fuses celestial grandeur with bodily effort, collapsing transcendence into sweat. The "twitters from a small bird" stand beside "dead male soul", a contrast between an innocent sign and a haunting presence. These juxtapositions create an atmosphere where mystery saturates the mundane. The poetess thrives in such imagery; the divine is never distant, but stitched into breath, labor, and sound.

The Literary devices are driven by paradox and personification. The 'tongue of serpent' embodies temptation, while 'gnosis' becomes a whispered riddle. Irony lies in the claim that wisdom must be both hidden and shared. The rhyme reinforces inevitability, pulling the poem toward its closing image of inspiration as both blessing and weight.

The Effect is reverent yet uneasy. Readers feel the beauty of divine touch while sensing the peril of misattributing its source. The poem closes not with certainty but with humility, a recognition that art is both a gift and a trial. This withholding of clarity is its power — the poem lets mystery remain intact, recognizing it as the most honest expression of inspiration's nature.

The Poetess: In the Garden of Eden, there were 2 trees -- for eternal life or forbidden knowledge of good and evil, the latter of which the serpent tempted Adam and Eve to eat. It is symbolic of the loss of innocence, possibly meaning the awakening of sexual knowledge and nudity -- the serpent as male phallic and the apple as female vulvic. They taste the fruit and are banished from Eden by God, who condemned women to painful childbirth and men to hard work.
(Pronounce realized as re'-lized.)

Poem 192: Dead Souls

Suspecting students used autom<u>atic</u>
Writing while watching him lecture in c<u>lass</u>,
Mister Roth assigned them, "In an <u>attic</u>,
Take a Ouija board. Spirit of the g<u>lass</u>,
Is a game for channeling me<u>ssages</u>.
Lay out the letters of the alpha<u>bet</u>."
"Sir, what if ghosts misspell words and <u>sages</u>
Do not make sense?" "I will wager a <u>bet</u>
That you will either show inte<u>lligence</u>
Or become confused, full of igno<u>rance</u>."
Next day, he observed their dumb di<u>ligence</u>.
They retained blank stares as if in a tr<u>ance</u>.
"Class, if the ghosts in a Ouija <u>session</u>
Are smarter, please allow their po<u>ssession</u>!"

Analysis Poem 192: Dead Souls

The Structure of the poem is staged like a classroom experiment, its rhythm clipped and didactic. Each line feels like instruction, alternating between the teacher's commands and the students' hesitant questions. The flow builds in staccato exchanges, giving the poem a cadence of a lesson turned ritual. The poem blurs pedagogy with séance, shaping the form of instruction into the mechanics of summoning.

The Meaning turns on the thin line between knowledge and superstition. A teacher's suspicion of dishonesty morphs into an assignment that flirts with the occult, replacing scholarship with spirit-play. The irony is sharp: students meant to display intellect instead collapse into blank stares, their pursuit of truth devolving into possession. The poem suggests that the hunger for hidden knowledge often entangles the seeker in confusion, where education mutates into invocation.

The Imagery is modest yet charged. "In an attic" conjures secrecy, a setting ripe for ghostly contact. The "Ouija board" and "spirit of the glass" bring immediacy, while "blank stares" and "trance" reduce the students to vessels rather than thinkers. The imagery is less decorative than functional, building atmosphere through sparse symbols that tilt the ordinary classroom into ritual space.

The Literary devices hinge on irony and dialogue. The teacher's wager — either intelligence or ignorance — becomes prophecy, fulfilled in neither success nor learning, but in trance-like failure. The rhyme binds the exchanges tightly, as if fate pulls the class toward possession. The final imperative, "please allow their possession" lands with chilling ambiguity: is it sarcasm or surrender?

The Effect is unsettling in its quiet turn. Readers begin in a familiar classroom but end in a space where intellect is eclipsed by the supernatural. The poem offers no release, only the eerie sense that the pursuit of wisdom may open doors best left closed.

The Poetess: One of the most intriguing occult tools is the Ouija board. It was made into a child's game by Parker Brothers/Hasbro in the USA. It has a reputation for being both good and evil, linking it to the subconscious and conscious, advising and perhaps, controlling people by possession. Using the ideomotor effect, it spells out words, letter by letter. My father said that while playing the Ouija board at university, it predicted he would marry my mother by spelling her name. They had already met as children once at her birthday party since their parents were schoolmates. I play it sometimes…

Finally, Sonnets to My Muses…

(Written especially for this book collaboration)

This is about my female muse -- my friend crush.

Pioneer in Court

Trained in law and order for judgmental

Decisions on life's family travails,

Attorney Alias experienced mental

Stress. Escape in territorial travels,

She pioneered women's equality

With PHD and law's feminism.

Marriage and motherhood gave quality

To her firm female determinism

To respect both career and family.

Up and down from the peak of a mountain,

She smiles, satisfied at such simile --

Like a balancing of scales can maintain

Peace, weighing values at home and in court,

See-sawing a spouse or legal consort.

For Attorney Amelia Alias -- until we meet again…

This is about my male muse -- one of my celebrity crushes.

Love Music Dreamer

Singing songs make his starry eyes sparkle,

Immersing wild fans in loving romance --

Female screams, yelling from heaven and hell!

PJ MacAmour band's songs make one dance,

Listening to him, their hearts' crazy cure.

His love lyrics are easy for singing

Foolish fantasies on an adventure

To sacred sounds of wedding bells ringing.

His songs remembered 'til eternity

Fulfilling females' frantic fantasies.

His wives agree that his paternity

Probably echoes concerts' ecstasies!

Like Apollo, a music god so fine,

He is a dream hero who could refine.

For PJ MacAmour -- and all your silly love songs…

Bibliography
Reference Sources of Original Works, Individuals, and History

		Pages
1.	Gerrymandering maps, Governor Elbridge Gerry, Boston Gazette 1812	12
2.	S.M.I.L.E., unattributed acronym for poetry analysis in schools	13
3.	Playwright and Sonneteer, William Shakespeare	13, 22, 25, 27, 33, 35, 44, 45, 217
4.	Crossing the Delaware River and the Battle of Trenton, Christmas 1776	18, 19
5.	Ending the War between Great Britain and United States of America, Independence of 13 state colonies, Treaty of Paris 1783	18, 19
6.	Authorship controversy, Stratford's Shakespeare or Oxford's Earl De Vere	22, 45
7.	Sonneteers: Francisco Petrarca, William Shakespeare, Charlotte Smith, Elizabeth Browning	25
8.	To London, to visit the Queen, Pussycat rhyme, Songs for the Nursery 1805	26, 27
9.	Head of the Commonwealth 1952 - 2022, Queen Elizabeth II	29
10.	The Elizabethan Age 1558 - 1603, Queen Elizabeth I	29, 45
11.	The Commonwealth 1949, ex-British Empire 1497 - 1997	25, 27, 29, 32, 33, 37, 39, 122, 123, 141
12.	Canada Constitution Act 1982, Independence of Canada from Great Britain	39
13.	American protest British Tea Act 1773, and Boston Tea Party 1773	43
14.	The King's Men 1603, Shakespeare patron, King James I & VI	45
15.	Royal Red Garter, Order of the Garter 1348	58, 59
16.	Cinderella, Perrault Tales of Mother Goose 1697	65
17.	Money makes the world go round, Masteroff, Kander and Ebb, Cabaret 1966	69
18.	G6 1973, G7 1975, G8 1997 - 2014, G20 1999 to present, Industrialized Group of nations	85

www.ingramcontent.com/pod-product-compliance
Lightning Source LLC
Chambersburg PA
CBHW080901120626
46555CB00008B/2898